Corporate Maturity and the "Authentic Company"

Corporate Maturity and the "Authentic Company"

David Jackman

Corporate Maturity and the "Authentic Company"

As part of the Business Law Collection, this book discusses general principles of law for the benefit of the public through education only. This book does not undertake to give individual legal advice. Nothing in this book should be interpreted as creating an attorney-client relationship with the author(s). The discussions of legal frameworks and legal issues is not intended to persuade readers to adopt general solutions to general problems, but rather simply to inform readers about the issues. Readers should not rely on the contents herein as a substitute for legal counsel. For specific advice about legal issues facing you, consult with a licensed attorney.

First published in 2018 by
Business Expert Press, LLC
222 East 46th Street, New York, NY 10017
www.businessexpertpress.com

ISBN-13: 978-1-63157-776-5 (paperback)
ISBN-13: 978-1-63157-777-2 (e-book)

Business Expert Press Business Law Collection

Collection ISSN: 2333-6722 (print)
Collection ISSN: 2333-6730 (electronic)

Cover and interior design by Exeter Premedia Services Private Ltd., Chennai, India

First edition: 2018

10 9 8 7 6 5 4 3 2 1

Printed in the United States of America.

Abstract

Corporate maturity is a valuable concept in that it provides a holistic view of an organization's performance, sustainability, and resilience. We present a general model of corporate maturity, which is applicable to any sector, with four main stages of development. We demonstrate how an organization can enhance its maturity through a focus on ethics, good governance, and community outcomes. We find that more mature organizations are those that find connections between corporate purpose and wider social and human needs. The authentic company, much in demand by investors, consumers, regulators, and employees is one that can be trusted to deliver these needs as result of deeply embedded integrity, uncompromising unconditionality and outcomes rooted in the community.

Keywords

authentic company, BS8904, corporate culture, corporate maturity, ethical space, ethics, governance, human maturity, ISO37101, risk management, social maturity, soft engineering, sustainable community standards, sustainable development, values-led

Contents

Foreword

The aim of this book is to establish the core concept of corporate maturity as a useful way of looking at the health, wealth, and potential of a whole organization and its associated wider "community." This concept may also be extended to include an "authentic company." We shall attempt of define "this form of collective maturity" in terms of the interaction between corporate, community, and social maturity. We will explain how the essential qualities of maturity and authenticity can be consciously and deliberately developed and measured. This will start from an identification of the many tangible and intangible benefits that accrue from being a mature and authentic organization, advantages that deliver results and improved quality of life for a wide range of stakeholders—including customers, employees, shareholders, investors, and suppliers. We shall, in particular, uncover the interdependent relationship between the maturity of individual businesses or organizations and the overall maturity of the wider community in which it is located (geographic or virtual) and the wider society it serves. Finally, we shall see how, especially in heavily regulated sectors such as financial services, maturity is a critically important charactersitic for regulators to be able to recognize, actively foster, and "reward" through regulatory dividends; while the maturity of the regulatory bodies themselves has intrinsic value for the success and advancement of the market systems they regulate. We will see how regulators need to develop in terms of their maturity in parallel and, ideally, at the same pace as the sector they regulate to ensure the effectiveness of the entire regulatory-compliance system.

This book does not seek to cover every aspect of organizational development or corporate governance, there are many existing helpful texts, but instead attempts to pick out those distinctive themes and sometimes elusive qualities that specifically differentiate mature and authentic organizations—and explain the unusual management levers and unexpected indicators that contribute to growing or nurturing a mature company or organization and their associated community. In part, this text is born out of a frustration with businesses' and organizations' obsession with the "quick-fix" and "silver bullet," or a cheap, simple, single-tool solution. We recognize that these are rarely successful or sustainable and so we find that we need to delve into the heart of complexity and accept the strength and limitations of sometimes partly intangible drivers such as integrity, unconditional commitment, and community cohesion.

Maturity and authenticity in practice are both robust and readily recognizable attributes to most people and at the same time sensitive and even delicate qualities that are difficult to artificially engineer or impersonate, almost impossible to force and all too easy to dissipate and fritter away. So much of their value depends upon keeping up a steady and unrelenting momentum that shows in solid day-to-day progress, some of which can appear uninspiring and yet which over time aggregates and can be seen to amount, often only in retrospect and perhaps with some surprise, to a very remarkable and worthwhile shift of substance. We are looking for substance over style, for differences of kind rather than of degree.

Finally, it should be emphasized that maturity is not a function of chronological age. This book is not about companies or organizations that have necessarily "been around for a long while," or been through difficulties. As we all know from everyday experience we can meet young people who are frighteningly mature compared to their elders. In the same way, young, innovative, and even disruptor organizations can carry themselves and behave in a "grown-up" and mature way and this will often prove to be a major asset in contributing to their continued success and longevity.

Most of all, corporate maturity is a direction of travel, for organizations and their regulators, as well as communities and societies as a whole.

David Jackman
Easedale
Grasmere
United Kingdom
March 2018

PART I

What

CHAPTER 1

Introduction

Corporate maturity is an overall, holistic view of an organization's health, wealth, and potential. Customers, for example, will often, if only intuitively, detect a "mature" approach that leads them to trust an organization and be more inclined to deal with it and perhaps become loyal to that brand. Similarly, discerning investors who look beyond the usual numbers and potential business partners may well be looking for signs of genuine reliability, resilience, and sustainability. They will calculate that an organization that is more likely to make sensible, wise, long-term decisions is likely to be one worth investing in. Similarly, employees may well increasingly be attracted to mature organizations that appear to have clear community-centered values they can identify with, and those higher quality employees may then be more likely to stay with a mature, and we might add, "enlightened" or "authentic" organization (expressions often used synonymously). And, importantly, regulators, government agencies, and international as well as national standards bodies, increasingly are judging organizations by the maturity of their culture and governance, rather than the processes and controls they operate. A mature organization can reasonably expect to develop a more balanced relationship with their regulators, which in itself can have immense financial and reputational value.

This book aims to:

- Explore the value of corporate maturity.
- Discover how maturity can be developed.
- Investigate ways of measuring and presenting maturity.

The same will be covered, in brief form, with respect to authenticity.

The arguments and methodologies set out here are applicable to companies of all types and sizes, in any sector or jurisdiction. The approach also works for noncommercial organizations, public and government bodies, charities, and the voluntary sector. This is largely a conceptual text but is based on extensive experience, research, and case examples from many sectors and countries.

We pay particular attention to the maturity of regulatory bodies as it is suggested that these should develop side by side with the sector that they regulate and at approximately the same pace to ensure both their supervisory effectiveness and in order to provide an enabling framework for the wider maturity of the sector.

As corporate life is an important part of many of our everyday lives and of our wider society, we also consider the interrelationship between corporate maturity and a broader social maturity. This becomes integral to the way in which communities develop, deepen, and build resilience and is, obviously, a two-way process.

Finally, we should remove any suggestion of a moral imperative here. Maturity does not necessarily equal a high moral quality, nor should any suggestion of immaturity mean necessarily "unethical," however, mature organizations, we suggest, are more likely to be conscious of their values, have them more carefully thought through and embedded ethics in their culture and operate what we shall term later, a system of "good" governance. Maturity is a collective state of mind, a set of characteristics and qualities, potentials, and abilities, and these can be exhibited in a small start up in an emerging sector as much as an organization that has been around for decades in a traditional sector. Freshness of thought and the ability to adapt are as much features of maturity as wisdom and endurance.

CHAPTER 2

What Is Corporate Maturity?

Corporate maturity is not a single concept. It is a compound of many contributing factors that intersect to produce a complex set of attributes. It is unlikely that all these factors are present or exhibited to the same extent in any one organization, but to conceptualize the presence of maturity it is necessary to hypothesize that a "mature organization" needs to have a critical mass of these characteristics and attributes at any one time to be considered overall "mature." This calculation allows for maturity to be developed and shown in different ways and so mature organizations may have different complexions. It also allows organizations to be just in the mature category or deeply mature and for any organization to slide backwards. There is no certainty that mature organization will remain so. In fact, it remains a constant task to continue development and sustain maturity.

Maturity is the result of a judgment about a combination of characteristics. In many ways, seeing corporate maturity is similar to the everyday judgment that we make when we evaluate the maturity of individual human beings. We frequently refer to someone being "mature" or behaving in an immature way, and the characteristics we are referring to in doing this are readily understood and recognized, and rarely, if ever, defined. It is an intangible whole, but one that most people recognize subjectively and place a great deal of importance of their judgment. It is the same in the case of our everyday and professional reactions to organizations and our overarching view deeply affects our understanding and appreciation of companies and their activities. We need, therefore, to allow ourselves to view organizations in the round and to find reliable ways of trusting these critical judgments. It really is an example of "the whole being greater than the sum of the parts."

What are these factors that combined to produce maturity? The following Table 2.1. sets out a comprehensive series of characteristics that are, by definition, closely interconnected and interdependent—and mutually supportive. It is not possible to be a completely inclusive list, and neither is it suggested that all factors are of equal weight in every situation. However, it would be unusual for a major category to be missing. The factors cited here are phrased in a way that applies to the maturity of the whole organization, but they also could, with minimal adaption, refer to the characteristics of the corporate leadership team, or, looking in the other direction, to the wider community of which the organization or business is part.

Table 2.1 Dimensions of maturity

Better quality decision making	Capable of seeing wider perspectives—wider community impacts, longer-term view, multiple stakeholders, multiple layers, ethical considerations. Combining many factors in a "rounded" way—drawing together disparate and disconnected factors draws from a wide variety of sources (each of which needs to be evaluated for their credibility and validity). Balancing different and competing interests—holding opposing views in tension. Able to deal with fine or close judgments and cope with multiple "grey areas"—and being able to identify the decisive differentiator. Being incisive and discerning what is really important to the organization and the community as a whole taking all stakeholders into account—that is, looking more deeply (we might call this *wisdom* and may refer to this as considering the "spirit" of the case, place, decision, and so on). These aspects in combination may be referred to as "Seeing the bigger picture."
Integrity	Holding on to principles and values or ethics under pressure and consistently, even when it is not in your interests and may cost the organization or individual something. (This maybe referred to as "doing the right thing" as opposed to "doing the thing right.") The organization and its staff are driven by internalized values, not just responding to external requirements or expectations (especially of regulators). This is not just tone at the top, or "mood in the middle" but embedded throughout the entire organization. Being able to use principles skillfully and, we may say again "wisely"; balancing what is practical and realistic and not being overly rigid, dogmatic or pedantic. Willingness to say "no" and to lose business or incur costs, if necessary. Being consistent, honest, coherent, and reliable in your position, product, brand, or service. We may say this is an *authentic business*—being genuine and true to your- or the business' "self."

Responsibility and fairness	Aware of who is depending upon you and who is your wider "community"—this sense of community may be geographical or virtual and may involve varying degrees of interdependence and mutuality. The rights implied or actual obligations are inevitably complex and involved. Meeting the rights and responsibilities of those who are involved or impacted by your decisions and actions. Holding on to a duty of care—defining what care looks like in practice. Fair and equitable—balancing internally and externally generated outcomes (considering the balance of benefits or costs for the organization and for the winners and losers). Open to others' interests and views no matter what their legal rights and interests may be and willing to take them into account—to a reasonable level—and to explain, discuss, and communicate your conclusions (which includes taking full accountability). Aiming to create consistent positive consumer and community outcomes—we will discuss how these are measured later. Having special regard for those who may be regarded as having special needs or being in someway vulnerable.
Empowerment	Creating sufficient "space" for individuals and teams to be able to make their own decisions. Reducing prescription to allow an element of self-determination and the ownership of decisions. Embedded values and a "pro-compliance, values-led culture." Flat management structures, short reporting lines, and reasonable, transparent, and nondiscriminatory salary spreads. Rewarding and communicating positive and cooperative behavior and habits. Inclusion, safety, and diversity as "normal." Naturally able to have "fun" and a sense of humor. *Note:* This section has an important connection with public accountability.
Learning	Investing in ongoing capacity building through planned, appropriately designed, delivered and progressive education, and not just one-off training, for example. Absorbing and acting upon positive experiences and also recognizing that mistakes and failures will occur and can be a valuable source of learning if properly evaluated, recorded, and relayed. Valuing all learning and finding feedback mechanisms for storing, sharing and accessing collective corporate knowledge. Seeing mistakes, criticism, and constructive challenge, for what they are, and not overreacting or introducing unnecessary sanctions. Embracing change in every respect. Making a positive, proactive effort to help others (and not just stakeholders) to understand your plans, decisions, and actions.

Accountability and openness	Willingness to explain and stand by your final and overall judgments. Ownership of decisions, short reporting lines. Not wishing to pass the accountability to others or split responsibility among many parties. Not obfuscating or resorting to "weasel words" to hide important realties. Not resorting to facile and legalistic defenses. Open as can be with as many as possible. Whistle-blowing both responsible and properly valued. Making information and reporting easily and freely accessible in a range of media and formats.
Confidence and attitude to risk	Confidence grounded in provable success and a matter of public record. Confidence of values, ethics, and convictions. Values not dependent on outside influences or the products of obsequiousness and gratuitous sycophancy, or self-serving self-interest. Willingness to openly challenge convention and assumptions, but positively and constructively with some notion of purpose. Having a balanced view of risk management, that is neither overly protective, nor reckless. Willingness to take measured risks to test out new opportunities, areas, or methodologies. Not dependent on others to underwrite or mitigate exposure in every eventuality. Having some authority, or gravitas, based on substantiated success and peer or professional recognition and public service.
Leadership	Facing up to pressing challenges and calling out the reality of the immediate situation (sometimes referred to as seeing the elephant in the room). Taking decisive action now, or as soon as possible, where required, rather than dithering or delaying and avoiding responsibility (often referred to as "kicking the can … down the road" or "… into the long grass"). Planning for the unknown futures. Consciously building capability and increasing resilience and sustainability thereby, within every decision and action. Willingness to share understandings and experiences with peers and competitors in a way that builds up the wider group, sector, and global community. Investing in innovation, not following the norm. Taking a long-term, independently minded, and broad-based view of imperatives of profit and reasonable financial return. Standing by principles and values when it is unfashionable or uncomfortable to do so. Ability to deal with deep ambiguity and widespread uncertainty and face "unknown unknowns."

	Willing to challenge accepted practices, assumptions (for example on compensation levels) and rules and break the mold. This forms part of "good governance."
Adaptability, inventiveness, and resilience	Willingness to be flexible and change your mind or direction, as circumstances evolve—at least to a reasonable extent. Capability, experience, and capacity built up sufficiently to enable resilience, that is shocks and surprises to be weathered or foreseen, and where possible mitigated or avoided. Investing significantly in research, development, and education. Ensuring preparedness, smartness, and strength through a variety of approaches and options, tools and methodologies, and maturity in depth. Capacity to seize opportunities as they arise or create opportunities and shape the agenda.
Transcendence	Reflective and an ability to answer the "why?" question. A developed "*sense of place,*" origin, heritage, culture, and rootedness—that is *belonging* to places, people, situations, and traditions. Ability to relegate self-interests and to commit to serving a wider interest, principle, or wider community. Good sense of timing, and sometimes "present" and sometimes "slow." Aware of supply chain provenance (fair trade, organic, local, sustainable, small business friendly, environmentally friendly, renewable, responsibly managed, recycled, up cycled, and so on). Building up our common humanity, with a degree of humor and common kindness. Understanding of "other" (however defined). Appreciation of the importance of human spirit and creativity. *Connectedness* to people, place, and principles. Vision of trajectory, authenticity, and place on the maturity journey (see conclusions).

Major Dimensions of Maturity Characteristics

These attributes are arranged in a logical order; some are intrinsic to the qualities of maturity, while a second group is more operational—essential to making maturity happen. Some factors "pull" the way in which maturity is shaped and developed, while others can be considered to be "push factors," driving the intrinsic nature of maturity. Consequently, it is possible to organize these attributes of maturity into three categories:

Drivers of Maturity

- Better quality decision making
- Integrity
- Responsibility and fairness

Facilitators of Maturity

- Empowerment
- Learning
- Leadership
- Accountability and openness

Outcomes of Maturity

- Adaptability, inventiveness, and resilience
- Confidence and attitude to risk
- Transcendence, connection, and authenticity

It is worth noting that other qualities, such as trustworthiness, respect, and authority often follow from the presence of these collective attributes and so might be best described as *derivatives* of the core attributes. How these qualities develop and combine is the core theme of this book.

CHAPTER 3

General Model of Corporate Maturity

It is important to emphasize that maturity is not achieved at point in time but develops and evolves. Consequently, the level of corporate maturity will change over time and, it is argued here, that while there is usually an inherent tendency or internal momentum toward an increasing level of maturity, this level may also fluctuate over time or even deteriorate and fall backwards.

Similarly, in developing maturity, organizations pass through a series of stages that lead to maturity. It is arguable that each stage is a necessary step. Some organizations never escape from the preliminary stages and we may refer to the sorts of organizations as being in various ways immature, or, to be generous, "not yet mature."

Core to the General Theory of Corporate Maturity presented here is an understanding of logical and progressive nature of these stages—each successive stage is the logical precursor to the next. Having established this pattern then we will be able to consider the mechanisms that develop maturity and identify reasonable and realistic interventions that can precipitate organizations to move from one stage to the next.

The concepts of corporate maturity inherent in this model follow a long philosophical, academic, and intellectual tradition. Jean Piaget's model of development in children (1932)[¶] and Kohlberg's cognitive moral development (1969)[**] suggest a cognitive basis for developing

---

¶ Piaget, J. 1932. *The Moral Judgment of the Child.* London: Routledge & Kegan Paul.

** Kohlberg, L. 1969. "Stage and Sequence: The Cognitive-Developmental Approach to Socialization." In *Handbook of Socialization Theory and Research*, ed. D.A. Goslin. Chicago: Rand McNally.

Kohlberg, L. 1981. *Essays on Moral Development. Volume 1: The Philosophy of Moral Development.* San Francisco: Harper & Row.

human maturity generally around moral judgment and decision making, especially in relation to wider society, its moral rules and expectations.[††] From this basis and many others, the author in a number of contexts has developed a maturity model over 30 years.[‡‡] The General Model is set out as follows (Figure 3.1).

1. *Minimum standards*
   - *Common question: Tell me what I have to do.*
   - *Repetitive transactional; get the job done, no questions, no sense of "why."*
   - *Simplistic, short-term financial goals, shareholder value excuse.*
   - *Oppressive and rigid hierarchical command structure.*
   - *Cynicism, do as I say not as I do.*
   - *Disenfranchising, don't take initiative, abdicate decisions/responsibilities.*
   - *Little or no connection with outcomes or purpose.*
   - *Alienating, undervalued, no desire to go extra mile.*
   - *No local connections or sense of place.*
   - *Turnover high, disposable staff on zero-hour contracts.*
2. *Compliance culture*
   - *Common question: What must you do?*
   - *Unthinking, mechanical compliance ticking boxes for comfort.*
   - *Routine treadmill—dysfunctional silo mentality.*
   - *Bureaucratic justifications and rote risk management.*
   - *Reactive to external pressures, firefighting; a culture of dependency on regulatory permission.*
   - *Frustrating lack of direction, unsophisticated measures of success.*
   - *Disconnect between board and frontline reality.*

[††] Trevino,L. 1992. "Moral Reasoning and Business Ethics: Implications for Research, Education, and Management." *Journal of Business Ethics* 11, nos. 5–6. pp. 445–59. Kluwers, Netherlands.

[‡‡] Jackman, D. 2002, 2004, 2015, 2016.

- *Fear infected—distributed sign off to avoid accountability.*
- *Time-serving—kept in the dark, petty rivalries, little thanks.*
- *"Outsourcing conscience" to regulator or consumer.*

3. *Business improvement*
   - *Common question: What can I get out of this?*
   - *Tokenism and posturing—vulnerable—gap between fine words and everyday reality for staff and customers.*
   - *Dull followers not leaders, incessant consultants' "benchmarking."*
   - *Improvements only based on a business case.*
   - *Possibly self-regarding and self-justifying; bubble of complacency.*
   - *Overexposed, vanity projects, pay inequalities.*
   - *Education secondary to competence "needs."*
   - *Ethics equates to a marketing edge, little integrity.*
   - *Staff policies and pay only to manipulate a result.*
4. *Values led*
   - *Common question: What do we want to do?*
   - *Independent judgment, internalize core values.*
   - *Spirit not just letter, beyond compliance.*
   - *Stakeholder balanced—long-term quality outcomes.*
   - *Well-developed individual responsibility, empowerment, and a sense of engagement by all staff.*
   - *Space to make and own decisions.*
   - *Wise, inspiring, "good" governance.*
   - *Sustainable and resilient, excellent environment.*
   - *Staff loyalty, engagement, and motivation add value.*
   - *Attracts best quality joiners, flexible working patterns.*
   - *Celebrates innovation, flexibility, diversity, and learning culture.*
   - *Worthwhile and clear purpose, answering the question "why."*

Figure 3.1 General model of corporate maturity[¶]

[¶] Jackman, D. © 2002, 2004, 2006, 2015, 2016, 2017.

The model describes four stages of development of corporate maturity for a single organization but this sequence can also be applied to an entire sector or an economy and society, as a whole. The stages are not watertight or mutually exclusive, but show a general set of characteristics that may be true of a group or part of a group.

Four Levels of Maturity

Corporate maturity both allows an organization to be evaluated and sets out a direction of travel, and an overall aspiration for that organization that draws together both commercial or other success and a wider positive contribution to society, community, and economy. These ideals will be developed in subsequent chapters.

Level 1–Minimum Standards: Here a firm could be just starting up or simply unsophisticated in its internal governance and culture, just doing as little as possible outside the core business model to ensure the business survives and satisfies any regulations or requirements to practice (e.g., licensing requirements–"pay to play"). It may operate "near the edge" and hope to "get away with it" and not be caught if it is in breach of any requirements or regulations. A firm may struggle to hold sufficient capital or maintain adequate liquidity to 'get by' from day-to-day and so might reasonably argue that anything else is unaffordable. It may well distinguish essential items from "nice to haves" and it may appear to such a firm that the qualities of maturity are simply luxuries. We hope to demonstrate that the qualities of maturity do not necessarily cost much or indeed anything at all and may well help to address current strictures and build the foundations of a successful long-term future. Some firms may see this level as a rational long-term position, keeping costs to the minimum and they may accept any consequent fines as an operational cost of doing business.

Level 2–Compliance Culture: Here companies are doing exactly what they are told to do by the relevant external body in a mechanistic, relatively unthinking and tick-box way. This is the position that too many large organizations find comfortable as it provides an approach that requires less discernment—simply the calculation is that with a large volume of compliance activity every risk must be covered somehow. These unimaginative and costly arrangements can appear to provide comfort, being the best way of minimizing all possible risk and ensuring the greatest degree of protection of reputation. It is also "safe" in relation to the herd mentality of keeping pace with competitors, although it is often here that sector-wide complacency can develop allowing the emergence of systemic risks—never to be properly identified or spoken about (as in the 2008 financial crash). Level 2 is usually the most expensive position to be in as organization overall, in terms of compliance costs and so is both risky and the least cost-effective place to be. This is the position where the common question of governance and compliance is more likely to be "show me where it says we can't…?" rather than "how can we improve our standards and conduct our business with integrity…?"

Level 3–Business Improvement: Developing maturity on the basis of a sound business case, may be seeing the component elements separately or often in their packaged form (such as in the form of corporate social responsibility, CSR)—presented as adding financial value and as contributing directly or indirectly toward existing business goals. But the danger of this level is that in pressured situations the business needs/targets may change and the financial case will fall away squeezing out such initial good intent. Level 3 is a stepping stone but can be a potentially fragile position that can back fire if the firm overclaims and then suffers a public ethical failure. This will cause a retreat to Level 2 or Level 1 and put back the course of maturity sometimes indefinitely.

Level 4–Values Led: "Doing the right thing" because you want to, not because someone tells the organization to. This is just the way you do business or run your organization. Arriving at this level is both an ethical and business commitment—the two imperatives, and others, converge at this point. In a mature organization key qualities and ethics are internalized, based on self-determined values that drive how business is carried out consistently throughout the organization. A truly values-led culture is a culture that is supportive of the aims and purpose of the business and the principles and values implicit in society, often mediated through regulation, and these values are subsumed within the firm's own values system, good governance, and culture.

The author has carried out a series surveys on the distribution of organizations across these four levels. The distributions do vary from jurisdiction to jurisdiction, reflecting another interesting feature that is the overall maturity of respective societies. However, in countries of higher levels of development the overall a general pattern of distribution might be:

Level 1	10 percent
Level 2	40 percent
Level 3	30 percent
Level 4	20 percent

The Maturity Curve

It is reasonable to suggest that it is necessary to pass through the pain and failures of the early levels and discover or experience the difficulties inherent at these stages before a more mature attitude and culture can emerge and become embedded. It is probably not possible to "leapfrog" to the end game or "skip" levels but there is insufficient data available on tracking organizational maturity.

The development of maturity is rarely a straight line and there are likely to be periods of slow evolution followed by more intense and rapid developments, even apparent "revolution" or transformation. This typical pattern may be described as product maturity curve (Figure 3.2):

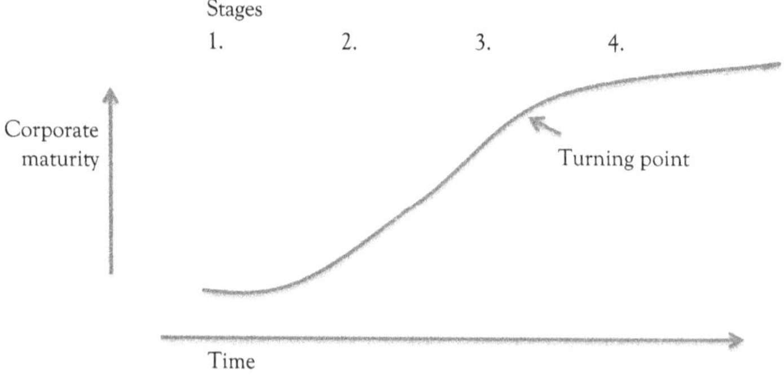

Figure 3.2 Typical maturity curve

In this typical corporate journey, the initial stages may be relatively slow as the basics of maturity are established. Once organizational internal capability, supported by any necessary external credibility, has been developed sufficiently there may well be a phase of expansion of maturity traits but sometimes this is not sustainable in the long term and the costs involved become counter-productive—so that a period of readjustment and consolidation can occur slowing the rate of change.

Level 3 to Level 4:The *Turning Point*

During Stage 3 there may also more fundamental changes in attitudes, values, and processes that allow a more thought-through, embedded, cost-efficient, and sophisticated level of maturity to emerge. Moving from Stage 3 to say sure is the most important and transformational. The stages before this can be regarded as preparation. The Stage 3 to Stage 4 "turning point" forms an important focus for much of the later sections of this book as we ask:

- What is required for this change in direction to be achieved?
- What exactly is the nature of this change?
- What are the implications of this turning point for the organization, its community, its regulators, and its stakeholders?

Once the *turning point* is passed the level of maturity may be more obvious, sustainable, and less costly to maintain. While it is always possible to lose ground, the embedded "credit" and momentum built up before this Stage 3 to Stage 4 turning point and the critical mass of effort, recalculation, and commitment necessary to move passed this point makes a later relapse to Levels 1, 2, and 3 less likely. Maturity has then become an intrinsic part of the whole.

CHAPTER 4

A Short Self-Test

You may wish to try to identify the level of corporate maturity of your organization. You can use this simple self-test.

Allocate the position of your organization along the seven dimensions shown in the following, categorizing the organization from level one to level four.

You can see at a glance the "center of gravity" of the seven positions you have decided.

This will give you an initial guide to the maturity level of the organization.

		⟵ 1	⟷ 2	⟷ 3	⟶ 4	
1	Ethics not prominent in everyday decision making					Ethics fully embedded, sometimes unconditional and may "cost"
2	Short-term financial goals or shareholder returns dominate					Long-term view, focused on balanced stakeholder outcomes
3	Limited connectivity with local community or environment					Mutuality and interdependence with community or environment responsibility
4	Hierarchical and siloed governance structure					Open, inclusive, diverse, flat, adaptive, smart and cooperative frameworks
5	Tick-box compliance and risk-management culture					Judgment based on "spirit" of principles, individual ownership and accountability
6	Reactive and dependency on external standards and interventions					Self-derived and internalized values, empowerment and constructive challenge, including an understanding of "why"?
7	Hire and fire regime, target driven					Long-term investment in people with a balanced scorecard approach recognizing a wide range of value added

Note: This is a summary of only ***some*** *of the elements and factors involved in corporate and organizational maturity and, therefore, the score is only an indication or summary and should be treated with caution.*

Maturity Profiles

It is very unlikely that all dimensions will be scored at the same level—in fact it would be unusual if they were. The pattern of your scores provides a company *maturity profile*. These maturity matrices can be much more detailed if you use more measures and they provide a route map for planning and evaluating subsequent development.

The matrix produces a profile that is, a zigzag line, not a simple pass or fail result (Figure 4.1). The profile will enable the organization to see what it is good at and to prioritize areas that are "lagging." In this sense it is a route map for progress and shows the steps for your further development. It is possible to see the "next steps" as a route map and plan on that basis. It could also be useful format for reporting.

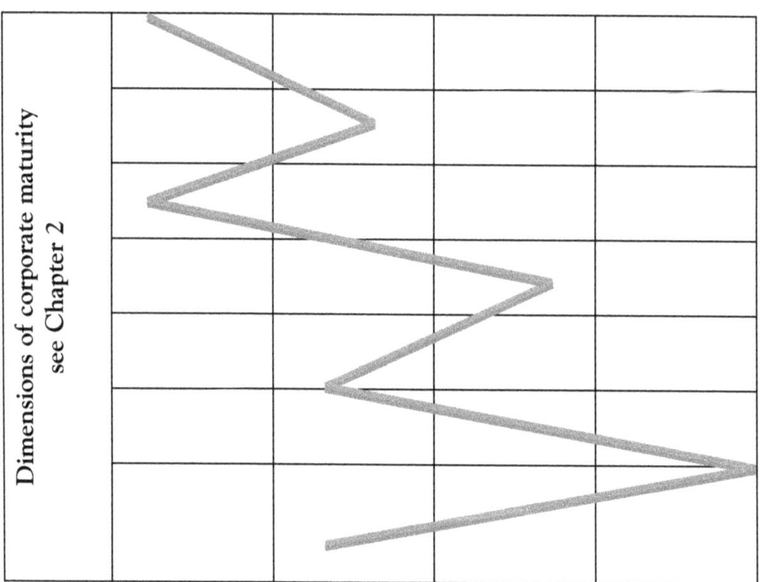

Figure 4.1 An example maturity profile

The following illustrates how the maturity profile can be set out:

Four levels of maturity.

This maturity profile can also be presented as a spider diagram with each spoke being one of the seven dimensions and the concentric rings showing the four levels of maturity (Figure 4.2).

In this hypothetical example the "Series 1" data might represent your starting position, that is, your benchmark, and then you might add subsequent datasets for each year's progress. Or you could map competitors' positions or use the system for allocating targets for future development.

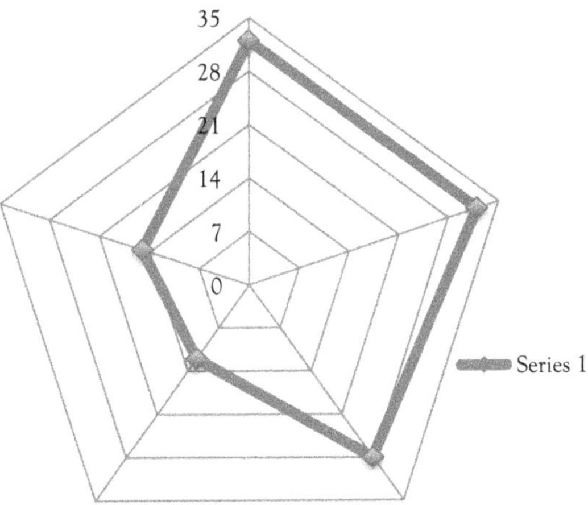

Figure 4.2 A spider diagram

CHAPTER 5

Business Case

Implicit within the definition of Level 3 is the suggestion that there is a strong business case for building maturity within a company (or even a not-for-profit organization) although this may not be a sufficient or even the fundamentally "right" case to drive development through to Level 4. We suggest that while a business case may be necessary to make the first few steps toward a sustainable maturity and authentic pathway, in order, for example, to secure early board support or targeted funding, it is rarely enough on its own to either justify or secure the entire journey to Level 4 and, in particular, to move any organization across the Level 3 to Level 4 tipping point or *turning point*.

A Basic Business Case

1. Reputation—immaturity can carry a significant bottom-line cost—and not only for one year. The "ripple effect" of being linked, or being seen to be linked, to an irresponsible action or unwise decision, or association, or situation can be very damaging and for other parties too.
2. Second, there is increasing pressure from the public and government to act responsibly in relation to the wider community and environments sometimes expressed as "put something back"—although it is much more than philanthropy. A good example is the growing interest in policies to combat social exclusion, inequality, and environmental damage. We will discuss the justification and implication of this these changing expectations in later chapters.
3. Consumers increasingly understand the elements of maturity which they may equate with being authentic, genuine, or having an ethical stance. These qualities may have general support or appeal to some specific groups of, for example, younger generation, consumers. This is part of establishing a license to operate, and indeed is differentiating between what might be termed "legitimate" aggressive

business strategy and unethical corner cutting which takes advantage of the customers lack of knowledge. The actions of one company may have a contagion effect. If consumers have diminishing trust in the sector in general as a result, they will hesitate to use the products and services of the entire sector, affecting all players.

4. If a firm that demonstrates maturity this can generate loyalty internally among employees and this is discussed in detail later. A more mature staff can in turn lead to early identification of problems that should result in cost and reputation savings for the firm. Clearly, a positive ethical stance as part of being mature has to spring from a genuine desire on the employer's part to promote higher standards of behavior—otherwise their efforts risk being seen as empty, manipulative, and opportunist in this could well undercut all attempts to improve maturity of the organization.
5. A sense of willingness in the sector to increase standards will, in some part, come from heightened interest to do so on the part of the individual organizations within the sector. However, when the efforts of many organizations are pooled, the impact can be cumulative and make a significant contribution to maintaining and increasing market confidence and customer engagement, that is, increasing sales. This could also help to absorb some "shocks" in the future.

Other benefits of maturity include the following advantages:

- Marketing edge—an improved brand image, trustworthiness, customer satisfaction, or reputation that increases sales, return, or revenue.
- Higher quality decision making and governance—allowing greater effectiveness and efficiency at all levels.
- More reliable empowerment of staff—greater alignment in values, vision, and evaluation—staff more likely to remain "on message" and deliver business positive decisions and outcomes.
- Greater attractiveness to quality recruits and lower turnover/improved loyalty due to more desirable conditions and meaningful work.
- Improved regulatory relationships—better standing and customer/market outcomes leading to a "regulatory dividend,"

experienced in terms of more manageable supervision, a closer partnership in policy development, improved risk-focused supervision.

- Attractive for investment—more reliable to investors, with higher long-term potential—leading to more secure and sustainable stakeholder relationships.

Business Case Research

The author conducted a standardized six-year review of the maturity of a cross-section of organizations businesses including a survey of all FTSE-100 firms (listed in the UK) and samples of corporations drawn from the Eurostoxx 50, the top 30 corporations in Singapore and the stock exchange in Ireland between 2009 and 2015. This research identified over 100 compound and interrelated measures of corporate maturity (benchmarked according to differing local regulations) and grouped scores under three headings:

- Compliance (with generally accepted governance standards and international and local regulations)
- Culture—capacity, reward, structural, and people dimensions
- Commitment—ethical, good governance, environmental, and community investment indicators

The data were collected from publically available information. The scores, however, also made some allowance for the quality, transparency, and openness of the reporting.

The headlines were published from time to time in the *Financial Times* (see bibliography), and some of the general trends observed were:

(a) Product regulated sectors such as engineering and pharma tended to score more highly then less-regulated sectors.
(b) However, financial services although being regulated in terms of conduct and service showed considerable variation in maturity levels, with the investments firms scoring generally higher than banks.

(c) There did not seem to be general correlation between maturity and firm size, or date of company formation, that is, age.

(d) Defensive sectors, such as mining and food production, seem to score either very well or rather poorly, depending on the jurisdiction in which they based.

(e) Straightforward compliance usually scored the highest subtotal, whereas commitment—possibly the closest indicator to overall maturity—was highly variable.

(f) In general terms, compliance scores increase over time in a reasonably settled pattern, whereas commitment seem to be variable and decrease in times of difficulty—supporting the suggestion that these dimensions may be seen as luxuries.

(g) The quality of governance seem to be jurisdictionally determined, with some jurisdictions clearly placing less emphasis on the importance of independence, committee input, board integrity, and reporting transparency.

(h) Environmental reporting is the most difficult area to standardize and compare with some jurisdictions offering or requiring considerably less transparency.

(i) There was identified a close correlation between return on assets and overall maturity.

(j) It is also possible to track over the six-year period the rise and fall of corporations as they faced various failures and embarked on programs of reinvigoration and reform. An example is Royal Bank of Scotland, RBS, which was undeniably in great difficulty following the 2008 financial crisis and at 66th place in these FTSE index rankings for maturity, but which, partly as a result of the impetus of government ownership, has risen to 6th place by 2015.

(k) It appears from a review of literature that a complex and compound basket of measures is at least as reliable, or more reliable, than identify a single measure of maturity.

(l) It is likely that, as reporting standards evolve, compound measures of maturity will become more reliable and the basket of measures could be evolved. The system did not change the basket of around 100 measures to allow for consistency and comparison over time.

CHAPTER 6

Costs of Immaturity

As we have seen some of the benefits of developing corporate maturity the opposite is true of failures, or a lack of maturity. There are costs of immaturity that can be seen in this cross-section of company and sector-specific problems, some that clearly resulted from low levels of corporate maturity and some showing more specific issues that seem to reflect poor maturity—and the levels of damage or loss of reputation—partly measured by fines incurred or loss of sales.

Examples from 2008 Crash

It is easiest, perhaps, to see the connection between immature behavior and poor outcomes and costs by considering the causes and consequences of the 2008 global financial crisis:

- The top 20 banks globally have been fined and charged a total of $321 billion since the financial crash of 2008,[*] the severity of which can be regarded partly as a function of the immature culture of certain individual firms and the sector as a whole.
- The fines are, interestingly, predominantly for cultural, conduct, and integrity issues (Figure 6.1):
- The then UK financial services regulator's the Financial Services Authority's (FSA) report into the Royal Bank of Scotland (RBS) focused on an "immature" board culture dominated by the then chief executive, Fred Goodwin.[†]

---

[*] CCP http://ccpresearchfoundation.com

[†] Financial Services Authority. 2011. *The Failure of the Royal Bank of Scotland: Financial Services Authority Board Report*, FSA, London. http://fsa.gov.uk/pubs/other/rbs.pdf

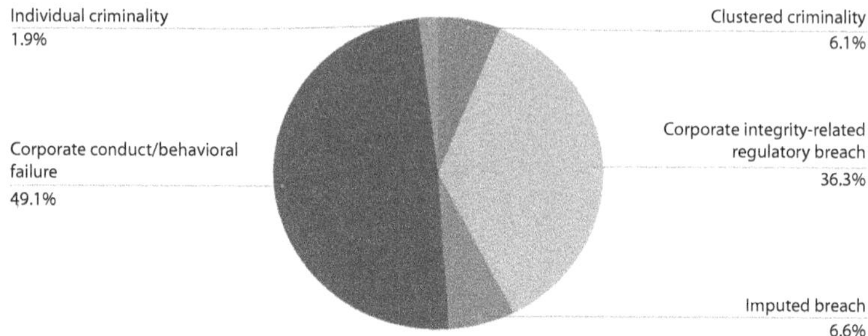

Figure 6.1 The composition of fines

Sir David Walker's governance review in 2009 that followed the 2008 crash listed 69 recommendations for improving the culture of governance in banks‡ and he understood that the failings were "more a matter of behaviors and culture rather than of organizational failings."

Other Examples

Automotive	20 percent fall in UK December 2015 sales	VW car emission violations
Press/media/film	Loss of titles e.g., News of the World and Bid for Sky under threat	2011 media phone hacking allegations 2017 numerous *New York Times*' allegations of pay offs to cover up inappropriate behavior at work in film and media companies
Retail	Repay £363 million	2017 BHS pension funds repaid by former owner, Sir Philip Green
Accounting	£214 million total fines	2017 Tesco's significant accounting scandals (previously, Toshiba and Olympus)
Textiles	13 charged with murder 17 firms committed to supply chain transparency changes by end 2017 e.g., Nike and Patagonia	2013 Rana Plaza 1110 deaths Child labor and appalling working conditions in the textile industry such as in Bangladesh

‡ Walker, D. et al. 2009. *A Review of Corporate Governance in UK Banks and Other Financial Industry Entities*. HM Treasury, London http://webarchive.nationalarchives.gov.uk/+/http:/www.hm-treasury.gov.uk/d/walker_review_261109.pdf

Tax issues	Loss of public trust Some boycotts	Corporate tax avoidance schemes, transfer pricing and "sweetheart" tax deals—including in the UK for Google, Boots, Starbucks, and Amazon who have been accused of transfer pricing through off-shore tax centers such as Luxembourg
Sport	Some criminal investigations	2015–2016 FIFA and IAAF alleged corruption Drugs allegations ongoing
Charity	Closed Numerous allegations of inappropriate behavior among relief workers 2018	2015 Collapse of charity Kids Company e.g., Oxfam officials in Haiti
Construction	Questioning of Private – Public Initiatives (PPI) in UK, penalizing directors and protecting pensions	2018 Collapse of second largest construction company in UK, Carillion engaged in many government contracts for hospitals, schools and rail lines. Into administration in January 2018 after several profit warnings in 2017 High profile political issue with considerable press coverage Some support offered to supply chain by five banks

It is difficult to say definitively that these are all a result of "immature" cultures but it would be hard to argue that immature attitudes and behavior did not contribute to the wide range of issues and sanctions that have emerged in businesses and organizations in recent years, of which this is just a sample.

PART II

How

CHAPTER 7

Five Elements that Develop Maturity

We shall consider five elements that create a "space" within which it is possible to cultivate corporate maturity. Each element is essential and points corporate entities or organizations in the "direction" of maturity (but not necessarily toward a defined outcome, for it is essential that they have to "find" the detail out for themselves) and these elements are necessarily interconnected, working in concert to weave an intricate "crucible" that positions and holds the entity in a pathway within which maturity is more likely to be developed. Within each element we identify several "levers" of change (from many that may be available) that can be utilized, by junior and senior management alike, to find corporate maturity. These selected key levers are considered in detail separately in subsequent chapters, but their effect should be considered collectively as they necessarily connect and interact with each other to be effective. Some specific tools or frameworks are also included in each element to help evaluate progress or, where precise measurement is difficult, at least generate useful feedback. It is also an underlying position that maturity can only be directed and consciously developed up to a point and that to a certain extent maturity has to be found "organically" by those involved so that they own, learn and internalize the maturity.

It is worth bearing in mind that this is a delicate process of "soft engineering" and so blunt instruments and heavy-handed interventions can be counter-productive. To balance this careful approach, there are moments when it is necessary to act decisively to overcome blockers and intransigent vested interest and in these circumstances independence within good governance is often critical. Guiding maturity is overall, perhaps, a balancing act of the intricate and the firm hand, more of an art than an exact science, or at least. We can see management of the maturity

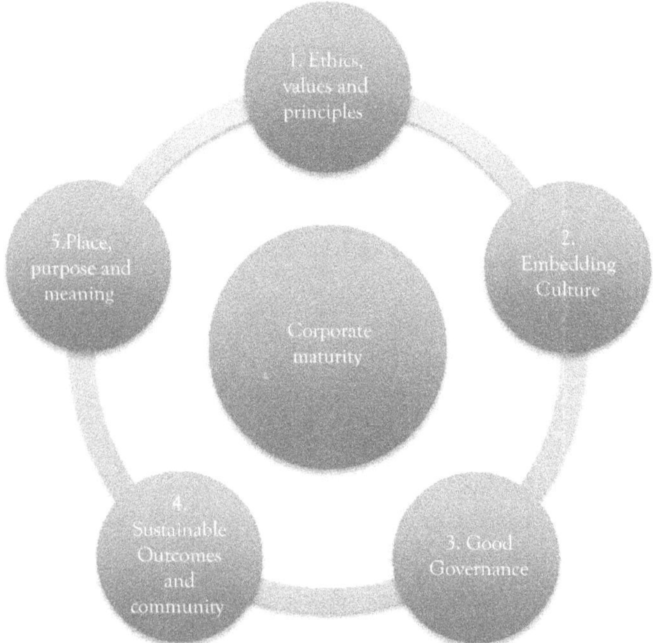

Figure 7.1 Elements developing corporate maturity

generally as akin to driving a vehicle, the right amount of steering and control is essential, but overreaction and sudden twists and turns can be worrisome. Intervention in this area requires considerable skill and specific competencies.

Each element contributes to creating the conditions for a lasting maturity. Is important to emphasize that they do not guaranteed maturity, that is to say they do not cause maturity, but they contribute to and allow the processes to emerge that generate and build maturity. These elements contribute to different aspects of maturity.

The elements' contributions are (see Figure 7.1):

1. Ethics, values, and principles—finding, unearthing or deciding the underlying drivers of maturity
2. Embedding culture—creating the structures or internal "ethical spaces" that are necessary to allow and foster the development of maturity

3. "Good" governance—the decision-making frameworks at the heart of "driving" maturity and being authentic for the long term. Authenticity is a product of maturity with an especial emphasis on consistent and evident commitment to ethics and values
4. Sustainable outcomes and community—measuring or evaluating the impact of maturity and its core contribution to ensuring the sustainability and success of the organization
5. Place, purpose, and meaning—cementing external connections and elaborating the role and place of the organization in wider society and the economy and understanding the meaning of work

These five elements themselves do not exist in a complete vacuum and we also need to consider how they operate within—and contribute to—the broader context of developments in maturity, specifically in:

1. Regulatory maturity (in a regulated industry, jurisdiction or sector)
2. Wider community and social maturity

We will consider these as parallel and interconnected developments and these help us to understand *why* maturity is important in Part III.

Spiral of Learning

Each one of the five elements considered earlier, to a certain extent, raises its inherent questions that are best answered by the neighboring element—so to be effective they have to be connected and the organization has to find those connections. To see the most logic sequence we will move around the "circuit" are five elements in a clockwise direction, showing how one element leads on to the next. For example, uncovering the values and ethics that are important to the organization very commonly leads to questions of how the ethics are to be embedded and "made real" in the everyday culture. These questions are normally operationalized within the context of the behavioral/cultural element, but the processes and structures that we see as essential to be developed within this framework almost inevitably raise questions of how decisions are made and how the accompanying risks are to be managed. This naturally leads us to a consideration of governance and given that we are working from an ethical base we might term the particular style of governance as "good" governance. Similarly, "good" governance cannot operate independently, without reference to critical externalities that revolve around a proper understanding the impact of the outcomes for individuals and the community in general, which, in turn, and inescapably are set in the context and dynamics of the place and purpose of work in society and our lives. It is this place that gives work meaning and can be detected as authenticity.

But the development of maturity is not only cyclical; although we recognize that when difficulties arise and growth slows (such as after 2008) it may well appear that way, at least to cynics. To continue from the earlier description, once the significance of community interaction is understood and absorbed there is a high likelihood of a reevaluation of values and ethics that will then set the circuit in motion again. Community and meaning, therefore, takes us back to ethics, as both reflect and shape our values.

In reality this is an interactive and dynamic process, with all elements interacting with all of the others, all of the time. To understand the complexity at a reasonable level we might conceive of an overall development cycle as a curative spiral of learning (Figure 7.2).

It is also important to establish at an early stage that this is not a sterile or academic model. All the elements described in this spiral are *active.* Organizations and individuals *practice* ethics, *live* and mould culture, *proactively* govern, *generate* outcomes, *deliver* on their commitments, and, to a meaningful extent, *commune* with a wider society and this journey

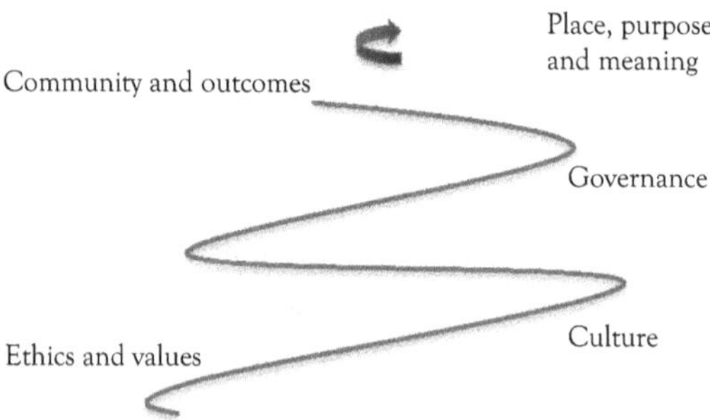

Figure 7.2 Spiral of learning for corporate maturity

creates meaning and purpose. This whole activity describes a constant struggle, sometimes a muddle, involving much trial and error, an evolving set of core questions and arriving at uncomfortable and uncertain partial answers—maturity is always a journey, and never a conclusion. Forging forward, sometimes in the "dark," consciously and unconsciously learning from experience, forever testing and retesting, hypothesizing, creating new approaches and solutions; the twisting the threads offered from the elements again and again is the essential theme of this book. And that creativity is part of the excitement and challenge of living and developing maturity for organizations and communities, just as it is for individuals. To identify the degree of maturity of any organization is to make a summation of the organization's *place* in this "journey."

CHAPTER 8

Ethics

Defining Ethics

We need to start this journey of increasing maturity by understanding what ethics are and where they come from. It is also useful to make the distinction between ethics and related concepts such as values and principles—all of which are linked and useful. This text will focus on the ethics as the prime descriptor of what the author has described elsewhere as a corporate faith—those things that any organization considers to be of the upmost importance.

- **Ethics** are the "goods" underlying all regulation and, thereby, compliance. The principles of justice, equity, and reasonableness are drawn from ancient traditions of ethics and philosophy. Some ethics may seem to be proposed by some (and in some situations) as absolute truths and at the other end of the spectrum some ethics may be regarded as entirely relative, contextual, or situational. This will be a matter of belief, ultimately—and that is OK. Society needs to have the degree of certainty to operate effectively and, therefore, tends to confer a more absolute sense to some ethics by incorporating them into the law and as human rights. Other ethics may be regarded as less fundamental to the structure of society or business life and therefore are able to be interpreted more flexibly and so are incorporated where necessary into legislation in a principle-only format. The balance between the rules-based and principle-based regulation is constantly under review and the position of the balance will depend upon the agreed needs of the society and the wider historical context. For centuries, the ethics of honesty, reasonableness and equity, for example, have underpinned many laws and form part of the accepted common legal infrastructure and so obviously find their way into the secondary legislation such as regulatory rules and guidance that affect most businesses and institutions. The ethics encapsulated in regulation are, thus, an extension of the essential ethics held by society, both formally and informally.

- **Values** can extend beyond ethics although the two words are often confused and can be used synonymously. Values is a general term for all of those concepts, positions on issues, generalizations, or beliefs that the organization decides (or believes) are important, and they may or may not have any ethical underpinning. Values tend to be a more practical applied word, not necessarily relating to intellectual philosophical position. Although values may indeed be ethical, they are expressions of anything that is important or a priority for an organization. Profitability and teamwork are values suitable for many organizations but are not necessarily based on ethics. We should also note that neither ethics nor values should be regarded as synonymous with morals which tend to be the more specific positions taken by individuals or societies on values and ethical issues, and may change from time to time and culture to culture.
- **Principles** are practical tools for the implementation of ethics and values. They are cited as general statements summarizing ethical positions drawn from a variety of sources, often considered together with case laws and other relevant rules that help guide behavior and decisions. Organizations and their regulators may use principles as a vehicle to translate desired ethics into everyday practice. Principles are "rules of thumb" that are meant to be flexible to cover as many situations as possible. They are useful in organizations and for regulators to avoid unnecessary and expensive prescription and are often the necessary counterbalance to rules and procedures. Where principles are derived from ethics it is usual to talk about the intent behind principles, often described as the "spirit" of the principles (and the rules based on them), in an effort to bring organizations back to underlying ethics without stating these

> ethics explicitly. Ethics and principles inform maturity and it also requires maturity to use these various forms effectively and intelligently.

Ethics, values, and principles all shape or influence:

- How organizations behave
- How customers are treated
- How committed staff are to the business
- The sort of people attracted to work in the organization
- How organizations are viewed externally (reputation)
- How effectively they can be run or governed
- Long-term sustainability
- Commitment in compliance

How to Define Your Organization's Ethics

This is the central challenge of this chapter.

The author set out to define the core ethics of one sector—financial services—for the first time by any financial regulator, for the then newly created single financial services regulatory body in the UK, the Financial Services Authority (FSA). These ethics were defined following a detailed trawl of the founding legislation of UK financial regulation, the Financial Services and Markets Act (2000), the FSA's Principles for Businesses and the Principles for Individuals, and other relevant international standards current at that time.

This new "Ethical Framework for Financial Services" was set out for the first time in an FSA Discussion Paper number 18 in October 2002.* *The* core ethics for financial services are set out in Figure 8.1 and these have formed the basis for subsequent retail initiatives focusing on ethics and culture, such as Treating Customers Fairly (TCF) in the UK and the Fair Dealing guidelines (to the Financial Advisers Act) in Singapore, among others:

---

* Jackman, D. 2002. *An Ethical Framework for Financial Services*—FSA Discussion Paper 18. London FSA.

- "Open, honest, responsive, and accountable;
- Committed to acting competently, responsibly, and reliably;
- Relating to colleagues and customers fairly and with respect."[1]

Figure 8.1 Core ethics for businesses

It is suggested that these ethics would serve as a useful starting point for any sector or organization. From this set, more relevant ethics could be derived that are closely attuned to the circumstances and the challenges faced by the sector or specific organization concerned. It is the process of discovery that is as important as the list created. And it is worth bearing in mind that the language used is also significant, in that any statement of ethics needs to be accessible and obviously practical for to have any traction and credibility.

The list is essentially a conflation of what may be described as core human ethics (such as honesty and fairness)—although this was not the conscious starting point—and these core ethics are supported by what may best be described as "contributory ethics" that give practical expression to the core ethics and buttress their general understanding and practical application (for example, openness and accountability help to prove or demonstrate honesty and fairness). To compile any comprehensive and definitive list of human ethics might be an invidious challenge because of the likely regional variations in interpretation—but we might chance that there is a cluster of related values that most people, whatever their circumstance or location, would recognize as being human "goods"—this might include general concepts such as honesty, fairness, responsibility, care for the more vulnerable, underlying security and safety, general liberty or established rights, representations and freedoms (such as those set out by the United Nations), the enabling and encouragement of creativity and expression, quality education and continuing learning, the celebration of diversity and mutual respect, common kindness, politeness, good humor—(that reflects a certain balance of perspective about what is important, the ability to put oneself second as reflected in self deprecation and the character to deal with mistakes and failure in an appropriate way), and decency. These, we suggest, are commonly shared core values that we hold by virtue of being part of the greater human family, not due to our culture or history or political habitats.

Ethics Codes

How these apply to any individual organization is often expressed in terms of a mission statement or an ethics code. This is a start. The steps you can take in setting up an ethics code (and some examples) are shown here for organizations that may not already have a set, but it is emphasized that accepting an externally given set, or one produced by consultants, is suboptimal and should be seen as a temporary measure. Nothing can substitute for an internally derived set of ethics as this is much more likely to be owned, understood and applied (and eventually treasured) by all levels of the organization. Once again, the journey is as important as the end result. There is no such thing as a perfect set of ethics and it is better to have a rough and ready set that is generally understood and owned, than a highly polished set of phrases, that may look impressive, but have little substance or connection.

Writing Ethics Codes

Key steps in setting ethics codes:

1. Develop a common understanding about what constitutes being ethical within compliance.
2. Ensure this aligns with regulatory expectations and business expectations.
3. Test your understanding with related departments such as legal and human resources (HR)—and in the line.
4. Gain board support, especially from "friendly" nonexecutive directors.
5. Pilot an ethical approach in a small area or division.
6. Roll-out to all staff.

7. Publicize or demonstrate to the regulator and other stakeholders, especially customers.
8. Continue to evolve, test, and update.

Common ethics codes might include phrases such as:

- We put our clients' interests first.
- Relationships of trust are at the heart of all we do.
- We always aim to "do the right thing."
- We deliver the highest levels of expertise and service.
- We make decisions on the basis of merit and principle; and stand accountable.
- We deal with decisions in an independent and objective way.
- We are rooted in community, fostering sustainability and prosperity.

Professional codes of ethics are more demanding in terms of personal responsibility and accountability. The following is an example created by the author for the International Compliance Association (ICA), the professional body for compliance officers.

The ICA Code

1. ...establish the "spirit" and intent of regulation and reflect upon its implications from the perspective of all key stakeholders, avoiding any over-simplification that diminishes the value and importance of compliance.
2. ...understand that the integrity and effectiveness of compliance is founded on independence of thought and judgment, recognising that they shall protect and ensure their independence and alert senior management or regulators should this be compromised. As such they need to ensure that they have a direct voice to the board of directors (or its equivalent).
3. ...take mature judgments in balancing competing priorities and conflicts of interest, interpreting "grey" areas, making fine judgements and decisions and then acting with the appropriate degree of sensitivity making difficult decisions when required to do so.

Behaviour

Compliance professionals must…

4. …be proactive in building a positive culture in their firm that understands, respects and is committed to regulatory objectives, values and outcomes.
5. …recognise that they have a unique and significant position with accountability to the firm and the relevant regulatory authorities, and must be clear and transparent about their responsibilities and the limitations of the scope of their accountabilities.
6. …be able to raise uncomfortable issues and ask challenging questions, making contributions that enables constructive challenge at all levels in the organisation.
7. …remain committed to open, clear, accurate, timely and accessible reporting, both internally and to regulators, and be committed to maintaining transparency as unconditional.

Development

Compliance professionals must…

8. …aim for open relationships with colleagues, offering high-quality advice and guidance, yet understand where ownership of risk lies.
9. …assist in the education and development of colleagues, undertaking regular briefings, inductions, training, horizon scanning, and compliance planning.
10. …develop their own competence, relevant to their role, through appropriate qualifications, training and continuous professional development and avoid exceeding the limitations of their competence.

A Critique of Ethics Codes

But this code is really disguised self-interest. It tells you more about the company than it may wish to say. Putting *"our clients' interests first"* is at worst unrealistic and disingenuous (it cannot be taken literally as the company would go out of business if it took this to an extreme) and perhaps at best thinly veiled marketing deceit. Surely a range of interests, including those of the customer and the company will be balanced in a mature way. Similarly, "Relationships of trust" cannot be demanded or delivered but are a product of such a mature relationship.

Another common claim is that organizations "do the right thing" (not just "doing the thing right"). But this tells us nothing. So what is "right"? It takes us no further forward than saying "I am being ethical" or "this is good." The interactions of many considerations are necessary, as we will see later, to have any determination of what might be ethical, right, or good.

The Trouble with Ethics

Ethics is a vague and robust term at the same time. In one, they combine the concept of overriding universal human shared values and the flexibility of interpretation and application in the context of a certain culture, context, and set of circumstances. The second character can seem to have the effect of undermining and devaluing the first, however it should not. Flexibility does not have to mean weakness or corruptibility, but can denote powerful universality and incisive precision. The trouble with ethics is that they are too difficult and we tend to be lazy; organizations prefer simple plug and play solutions and there is rarely the capacity or appetite for hard work without certainty of valuable outcome. Maturity means corporates having to learn to deal with nice distinctions, with fine and delicate lines that so often turn out to be really important and visible to the public, to investors, to regulators, and so on.

Another way of making progress is to widen the pool of individuals and groups involved in the discussion—this is the widely understood stakeholder engagement process. This is widely covered in corporate social responsibility (CSR) literature[†] but it is worth noting at this early

---

[†] ISO 26000 is the widely recognized corporate social responsibility International standard, contributed to by the author.

stage that while CSR is to be generally encouraged, CSR is no substitute for having an ethical core or being values driven in all the organizations activities and behavior.

We have emphasized that the journey is probably much more important than the finished product. And anyway, a valuable ethics code will constantly be reviewed and revised so there is no finish product. To provide some practical help in starting on this journey and uncovering what an organization may decide is it's ethics, we suggest the following exercise using an established tool to prompt discussion and provide a framework around which individuals and other interested parties can get together and sort out what could be included.

Your Ethics Statement

Introduction

Ethics cannot be measured so this is a framework to help organizations to explore and uncover what their values and ethics might be. It forces senior leaders or teams to surface and commit to a set of statements that represent your ethical views and position.

You should end up with a statement that you are willing to be public and shared, it is a not a private matter. You should have the courage of your convictions at the end of the process because, in part, you will be clearer about what you think and what is important to you—collectively.

This can be painful, slow and taxing—it is meant to be probing. It may at times and in places be driven by inspiration or be inspirational, that is fine, but if it is not that does not mean it is less valid.

The sections contained in this tried and tested framework broadly relate to the chapters of this book and so it may be best to try to complete this exercise only when you have finished all the Part II chapters. However, it may also be sensible to try the discipline it creates now as that will inform how you read the remainder and then come back and rewrite if needs be. A quality statement is often an iterative process and it should also be a living document often revisited and updated.

Your Values Statement

The questions are intended to be open ended so that you can better express your values without being restricted by a rigid framework. Some of the questions may be difficult to answer so we have provided guidance notes.

There are no "right" answers, since the aim is to tease out how your organization meets its ethical challenges, presenting a very real and honest portrait of your organization and the shared values that it represents. Since the ethics is not just about process, but also about commitment and outcomes, we require that you address all of the key ethical issues that affect your organization, both as a measure of your sincerity and in order to identify areas which you may need to develop in the future. It is important to consider as much evidence as possible to support your statement.

Motivation or Purpose

Why Do You Do What You Do? What Drives Your Actions and Plans? What Are You Trying to Achieve?

What is the purpose of your organization? What is the wider impact of what you do? Why is it worthwhile? Mission statements abound but how do you express the aims, direction, and value of your organization and enterprise? What really drives your organization? How do you strike a balance between, profitability, shareholder return, employee fulfillment, consumer trust, and community commitment?

Impact on the Environment and Community

What Are the Economic and Social Outcomes of What You Do—Both Short and Long Term? What Steps Have You Taken to Reduce Your Environmental Footprint? How Do You Benefit the Local and Wider Community?

Organizations can have a profound impact beyond their immediate stakeholders. When considering the outcomes of what we do, we therefore need to be mindful of the wider implications. What do you regard as your community? How do you contribute to building capacity and resilience? Can you explain your approach to sustainability and the practical actions you have taken?

Engagement and Embedding of Values

To What Extent Are Your Values Embedded in the Culture of Your Organization? How Do You Involve Your Stakeholders in Understanding and Engaging with Your Values?

How widely are your values understood and shared? How are your values incorporated into top level decision making? How do you develop your values and create the space in day-to-day working practices to do so? Do your reward systems reflect your values? How is your organization engaging with and involving stakeholders in decision making and planning? What steps are you taking to educate, train, and motivate your staff on your values? What, if any, steps are you taking to be inclusive and to deliberately help others to understand, your position, your values, and the reasons behind your decisions?

Relationships

How Do You Treat Individuals and Organizations As They Would Like to Be Treated? How Do You Demonstrate Fairness?

We would all like to deliver the sort of service that we would like to receive ourselves. Companies are often conscious of the customer and those to whom the company is accountable. How far down the supply chain do you feel responsible? What level of due diligence is appropriate?

We are unlikely to be able to satisfy everyone, all of the time. If you target a certain market you may well exclude or offer an inferior service to some people. Is this right, or is it something your organization needs to address? We all make mistakes, but far more is revealed about us by how we deal with them. How do you deal with the inevitable mistakes, complaints and concerns?

Ethical Pressures

How Do You Specifically Use Your Ethics in Dealing with Conflicting Pressures? What Are the Practical Constraints or Barriers to Developing Your Ethics? How Do You Make a Direct Link Between Your Values and Your Actions?

We may face opposing pressures in our business life—quality, cost, return on investment, integrity, deadlines, environmental impact, work or life balance, and many more. It isn't always easy to reconcile our obligations to different parties. Given these conflicting pressures, how do you deal with them as an organization? What challenges do you face in balancing the demands of different customer or other stakeholder groups? Can you show a direct link between your values statement and your everyday policy making, decision making, and actions? Can everyone see this? Are you happy to "own" your decisions? Do you make "brave" decisions?

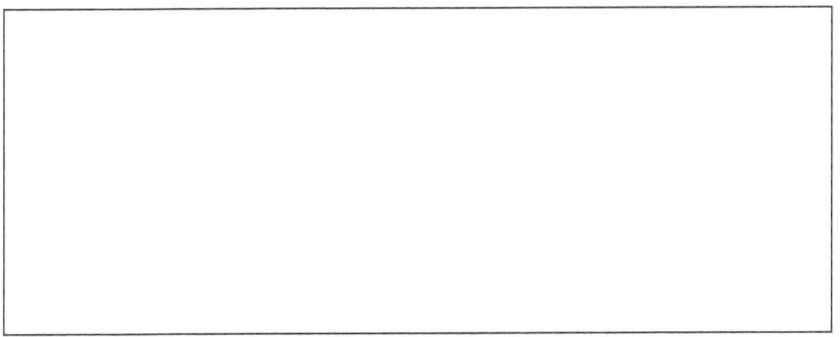

Leadership and Authenticity

How Do You Provide Leadership in Ethics? Who Do You Inspire? How Do You Demonstrate Your Authenticity?

How do you take a stand? How do you innovate or push the boundaries in respect of ethics? In what ways do you seek to influence the values of others and the ethics climate in which you operate? How do you develop employees to their full potential and how do you build understanding and skills in others? Whom do you motivate by what you do, or by how you do it? What are you wanting others to see you are committed to and how is this evident in the running of your organization?

Embedding Ethics

Ethics may be now a familiar subject. But this was not the case in 2002, when the FSA initiative cited earlier was regarded as groundbreaking, innovative, but also troublesome to a degree. In the intervening time there has been a revolution in the approach to ethics as it has become apparent through a series of crises—Enron and WorldCom, the global financial crash, rate fixing, the Siemens, Toshiba and VW cases, and endless mis-selling scandals being the most obvious—that poor ethics has underlain unsatisfactory corporate behavior and considerable public disadvantage. Responses have often been short-term, knee-jerk reactions and these too have been exposed as insufficient to fix substantive ethical problems. Window dressing or whitewashing is clearly not a long-term solution. Many organizations have been unclear as to what to do. This has allowed such organizations to misdirect their resources with considerable effort expended on devising ethics codes, running ethics training, and reporting on ethical indicators. None of these are in themselves unhelpful, but on their own they are likely to be ineffective and even counter-productive. Consequently, despite these noble sounding advances ethical "lapses" still occur on a regular basis. Indeed, it may seem to the casual observer that such lapses have increased since the milestone of the 2008 financial crisis, which the public in general might reasonably have regarded as a final and incontrovertible lesson to any organization, although it should be noted that the impression may be exaggerated by the normal phenomenon of increased reporting that results from growing public awareness and therefore improved reporting standards.

Certainly any organization's conception of "ethics" should not be not "fixed" or time bound—there is always room for improvement and evolution. So having an existing ethical code or statement should not bar an organization from revisiting the area and make you more determined effort. The fundamental question remains for all organizations that arises from any consideration of ethics is: *How can corporates properly understand and then embed ethical values in their day-to-day operations in a way that is effective, consistent, and sustainable—and that adds value to the business.*

The challenges in this area are:

1. Finding and understanding the subtleties of ethics, values, and principles such as integrity beyond the simplicities of usual corporate discourse.
2. Establishing a range of more effective and sophisticated ways of embedding ethics sustainably in a corporate structure.
3. Ensuring that ethical judgments are not undermined or overridden by apparently more immediate and powerful concerns.

These questions naturally lead us to the second element of embedding ethics in the everyday—culture.

Note

1. Jackman (2002).

Reference

Jackman, D. 2002. FSA Discussion Paper 18 An Ethical Framework for Financial Services.

CHAPTER 9
Culture

Creating the structures and "habits" that enable ethics to inform maturity.

What Is Culture?

Culture is the values, ethics, attitudes, habits, assumptions, heritage, expectations, and aspirations that shape our everyday actions, decisions, and strategies. In any company there are collective elements of culture embedded in the fabric of the company's "heart and soul." But we are not passive in this. Our work is shaped by the corporate culture but we can also help shape it—we are all part of corporate culture and have a responsibility for it and what it delivers.

Culture can be said to exist within a company, a sector, and the industry as a whole. Some elements are local and others global, coming from accepted practices and centuries of interaction between centers and institutions. However, while some elements seem relatively stable other elements of culture can change or be changed remarkably quickly. Culture may change from within as, for example, new management arrives, or as a result of external factors such as public or client pressure, changing economic circumstances, crises, and government policies. Internal and external factors working together usually are highly effective in shaping and reshaping corporate culture.

If you can alter culture, even slightly, you will by definition affect the way everything is done subsequently in the company, the decisions at every level and the outcomes of the company and sector.

Culture and Maturity

The importance of culture in maturity is the structures embedded in all aspects and levels of the organization that generate decisions and foster certain behaviors, attitudes, and habits. It is these sometimes delicate, sometimes robust, or even entrenched structures that need to be identified, consciously engineered, reengineered, or deliberately implanted to produce and maintain cultural change. These need to be managed consistently injected into all aspects of corporate life—in a process we shall call "soft engineering."

"Soft Engineering"

Soft engineering is perhaps the most cost-effective way of achieving maturity and managing a business in many other ways for the long term as it *directly* addresses the levers and conditions that create and shape decisions and actions. This is intervening to deal at source with the root cause of success and failure and organization wide conduct. It is, therefore, also key to managing conduct risk, regulatory relationships, and overall maturity.

Advantages of soft engineering:

- Deals with fundamental causes that affect the entire corporate character and operation.
- The most cost-effective lever for change (Interventions further down the decision-making chain may need to be more substantial and difficult to embed).
- Immediately understandable—connects with the everyday experiences, priorities, and issues of customers, staff, members, the media, shareholders and increasingly, regulators.
- Directly relates to conduct risk and consumer outcome.
- Unites intention to action that is, it provides a rationale for values, standards, decisions, and measurement.
- Offers answers to the question "why?"
- Shared assumptions underpinned systemic failures, including the 2008 financial crisis.
- Cross-cultural and evolutionary.
- Principle based allowing for the flexible interpretation and implementation.

The focus for developing culture is creating the "space" for maturity. This as much about allowing, trusting and empowering people in organizations to make their own decisions as guiding them or instructing them in making an ethical direction.

Key is the appreciation that decisions made by individuals themselves rather being prescribed "top-down," or by external bodies such as regulators, are more likely to be "owned," and it is more realistic for those individuals to understand and play their part in accepting appropriate accountability. This empowerment is a more mature working style than a conventional, and more immature hierarchical command structure—as may be observed in wider aspects of life. Maturity requires treating people maturely and enabling them to be mature in response. Shaping culture to achieve this in a careful and measured way is a form of engineering but also something of an art in its complexity. Success requires many different components to come together, but at its heart maturity requires consciously being human.

Key to the process of developing maturity is creating "ethical spaces"—or bounded scope for taking responsibility—by removing or reducing layers of prescription in an ordered, progressive, and careful way that gradually increases the degrees of freedom for staff. This must be done knowingly with:

- Full communication with staff involved
- Firm boundaries (hard rules) that still cannot be crossed
- Rewards and appraisals recognizing progress—with any necessary sanctions that are reasonable, equitably applied, and communicated
- Support in the form of guidance, mentoring, ongoing education, and gap-filling training
- Open and regular measures that tell everyone how they are doing
- Case histories that recycle valuable experience and provide a log as reference for learning from good and bad experiences

This greater freedom increases the likelihood (but does not ensure) that individuals and teams will step forward and make "ethical" decisions. But they might not, this concept rests in part on your view of human nature, and so there needs to be enough structure to enable the organization to either limit risk or step back in if problems are emerging or if the release of constraints is too fast.

This winding back of prescription, stage-by-stage, is a learning process for everyone and is not indefinite. There is an optimum level where the advantages of greater freedom are nicely counterbalanced by the disadvantages, risks or costs of freedom, and the advantages of control. In effect you may be increasing to an extent people risk to manage risk more effectively and to allow maturity.

The Importance of Learning

Maturity develops over time as people understand better the freedoms and constraints of their role, based upon the values underlying their business and wider ideas of good and right inside and outside work—that is, ethics. Maturity takes time and is akin to the wider learning experience. In fact it could be argued that an attitude of openness to new ideas and to learning is essential for a maturity to take root, to grow, and to be effective. Only by engaging in the process of learning will anyone be bought-in, committed, and engaged. Once engagement stops other influences will emerge and the maturity can dissolve quickly. So constant work, with influences on staff converging and support by the right kind of infrastructure is required to maintain a compliance mindset.

Examples of Failing to Learn

Example 1: Some indicative extracts from the Financial Services Authority's (FSA) Report on The Royal Bank of Scotland (RBS) referring to aspects of maturity include:

Para: 575

> Some aspects of management, governance, and culture can be assessed fairly precisely. For example, it is possible to identify whether a bank has appropriate formal processes of governance by reviewing matters such as whether board agendas cover appropriate issues and management information flows to the appropriate level.

However, many of the important questions about management, governance, and culture cover issues such as boardroom dynamics, management style, and shared values. These, by their nature, are matters of judgment and are difficult to assess precisely, even on the basis of contemporaneous documentation. For example, assessing whether key board decisions were subject to adequate monitoring and challenge is inherently difficult, as the minutes of board meetings typically record the decisions taken rather than the detail of how or why a particular decision was arrived at, or whether alternative views were expressed in the course of the debate. And assessing a firm's culture effectively is difficult even when done contemporaneously, let alone when attempting to assess the past. Despite these difficulties, the Review Team has concluded that it is highly probable that aspects of RBS's management, governance, and culture played a role in the story of RBS's failure and should be addressed in this Report.

Example 2: Barclays' Saltz Review*

Banks in particular are built on trust. After all, they look after our money. Banking requires that we have trust and confidence that our bank is not taking undue risk. Building an organization's reputation for trustworthiness takes time and is founded on a robust ethical culture supported by leaders, systems, and policies designed to foster and reinforce employee trustworthiness. In industries that are associated with risk and risk-taking, the work that must be done to establish and sustain trust is greater. Barclays' work on culture and values comes at a time when trust in banking and bankers is at an all-time low. Trust comes from an expectation that what is said will be delivered. Trust is also strongly related to fairness. Studies show that the experience of unfairness quickly erodes trust.

---

* https://online.wsj.com/public/resources/documents/SalzReview04032013.pdf

... Values drive everyday behavior, helping to define what is normal and acceptable, explaining how things ought to be (for example, staff ought to put customers first). Values provide a framework through which the natural and often difficult conflicts that arise in people's day-to-day work can be resolved. But they will not always provide the answers. Organizations need to create an environment where employees feel it is safe to resolve the frequent differences that arise. For example, on a daily basis, retail bank staff can face the dilemma of determining which deposit product best meets customer needs given the frequency with which interest rates and conditions can change.

... there is a significant challenge to instilling shared values in a universal bank like Barclays. Cultural compatibility is difficult to achieve across businesses that may attract very different employee profiles, and where the business model and objectives are different. It takes a great deal of finesse to translate the same common values into credible expectations of a trading floor and of a retail branch network. This task is made harder when, as at Barclays, rapid growth (which propelled it from a family bank to a leading universal bank), multiple reorganizations and extensive external hiring (particularly in the investment bank) create a less stable cultural base.

... Our review of the performance evaluation documentation revealed little emphasis on culture and values. Where present, there was little evidence of how the performance evaluation process used values effectively as a means to drive behavior. For example, in the investment bank, although "integrity" was specified to be a key value, the performance evaluation parameters used to determine integrity (even in relative terms) were ill-defined. The crux to embedding values is as much about the zero-tolerance for value breaches as it is about determining what good looks like. Some of the failures to report and escalate poor behaviors relating to the LIBOR (the London Inter-Bank Offer Rate—the baseline interest rate which is set daily and on which many other rates are based such as mortgage rates for retail customers) issues demonstrate quite how loosely certain values were applied.[†]

Constructing Crucibles

The concept of "crucibles" or frameworks is useful to understand how to provide the necessary structure for maturity. Senior and lower levels of management need to construct these crucibles within an organization and manage them. The concept of the crucible brings into play the twin elements of freedom of decision and action within a structured or pressured container.

In general greater maturity requires more elaborate, carefully constructed and ubiquitous crucibles—providing the reliable and consistent opportunities and structures necessary for cultural change and constructive challenge. These should be deliberately built within everyday decision-making procedures so that they contain everyday situations and processes that explicitly and directly encourage individual and collective questioning and quality deliberation, within carefully risk-controlled, boundaries.

Components of the crucible (see Figure 9.1):

1. "Base"—Foundations of ethics, values, and principles that emerge from the explorations are described in Chapter 8. Together these form the drivers of maturity and are essential, but may evolve over time. The connection with place, purpose, the environment, and community will be explored in subsequent elements.
2. "Lid"—The sense of direction, trajectory, purpose, and role that develops from and with the ethics and values of (1) but also provides the necessary momentum which may well be expressed in terms of vision, "mission," objectives, and more specific targets.

[†] Walker, D. et al. 2009. A Review of Corporate Governance in UK Banks and Other Financial Industry Entities. London: HM Treasury. http://webarchive.nationalarchives.gov.uk/+/http:/www.hm-treasury.gov.uk/d/walker_review_261109.pdf AQ: Please provide the Remaining author name instead of et al.

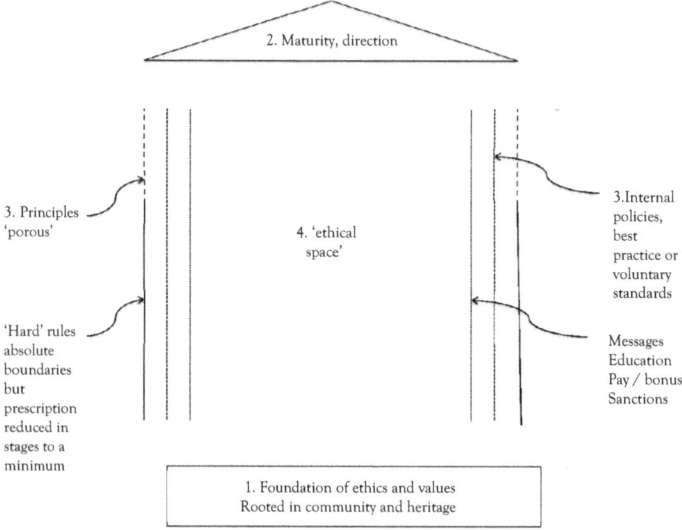

Figure 9.1 The structure of a crucible

3. "Walls"—These are the very necessary constraints all boundaries that keep decision making on track and moving in a positive direction. These boundaries may consist of "hard rules" or policies, creating absolutes that should not be crossed. Gradually some of these may be able to be replaced by more porous and flexible principles which allow for increasing degrees of discretion and may well accommodate technological change or uncertainty and allow more easily for changing circumstances. These hard and soft boundaries may need to be supported by appraisal, reward, and sanction policies and policies, procedures, messaging, and education. It is likely that such reinforcement needs to be more proactive and obvious in the early stages and can be relaxed overtime as staff or colleagues become more used to the intentions and ethics underlying the direction of travel. In fact, is likely that if these conditions are not relaxed overtime they can become obstacles to further progress and the further stages of maturity could appear irrelevant and unattainable. This will reflect poorly on management and undermine the necessary relationship of trust that underpins this stage and the sanctions and rewards that are required for it to be effective and supported.

4. "Ethical space"—This is the essential component and is the space within the center off the crucible that specifically is left clear of centralized top-down prescription and allows for individuals and teams to look for their own suitable inputs and consider a variety options. This ethical space is also part discipline, as staff and colleagues, while being empowered to make their own decisions (up to a point) also understand more easily that these are decisions that they quite reasonably own and therefore should be accountable for. This finesse requires prescription to be removed or relaxed in stages and over a defined period of time so that predetermined "right answers" are withdrawn or are not always available. Without removing these rote answers provided by the usual levels of internal procedure and policy and reducing the level of audit style box ticking, staff will remain dependent and will not mature and gain the essential sense of responsibility.
5. Applying "heat"—By provoking higher quality and more regular constructive challenge—to the staff or colleagues in the crucible has a tendency to encourage and to an extent force the development of corporate maturity. This heat can consist of constructive challenge (as we will see in the next chapter), together with communication of positive and negative experiences, continual training, and education including the logging of learning and leadership that "walks the talk" both internally and externally.

Engineering such a series of structures within an organization's culture in this way is not about "precooked" solutions, with set cultural norms overly defined, or the creativeness of the process is lost. Even worse is a system of "nudge," coaxing staff toward solutions or decisions—which could appear in a crucible process as deceitful and corrosive. This is about opening debate to all and empowering everyone in everyday situations, making decisions, dealing with a complaint, setting a strategy, mending a problem effectively, and for the long term because there is self invested in each decision.

Crucibles are designed to create an environment where difficult issues and questions are raised regularly so that they become part of everyday, normal conversation and culture. Everyone will build confidence and competence in handling these issues and it will be clearer what you define as being acceptable or not.

Culture as "Glue"

Culture is the glue that binds individuals to an institution; it creates a consistent framework for behaviors and business practices. Culture is what people do when no one is watching—indeed, "desired values and conduct should be reflected in the daily habits and practices of employees—how they work; how they are evaluated; who is hired, promoted, and rewarded; and how employees act when managers are not present and when matters of personal judgment arise."[‡] It is possible to construct such genuine structures on a human scale and within corporate processes to develop ethical culture.

Initial Self-Test

This exercise will help start a conversation or an investigation into corporate culture.

To what extent do the following processes contribute to maturity?

		None		Significant	
		1	2	3	4
1	Consistent and regular communications				
2	Opportunities for learning, qualifications and development				
3	Specific rewards for ethical or mature behaviors				
4	Adding to prosperity, innovation, or job creation				
5	Supportive "tone from the top"				
6	Connections with community				
7	Work-life balance Flexible roles or team spirit				

‡ G30 Banking conduct and culture: A call for sustained and comprehensive reform, p. 12, 2015.

8	Worthwhile outcomes or a "good" cause or sustainability or legacy				
9	Empowerment and space for constructive challenge				
10	Company values align with personal				

This will give you a score out of 40.

Having scores of 3 or 4 for each line suggests maturity. The pattern may not be even, so we could consider that an overall total score of over 30 could be considered an indicator of a "mature" culture.

CHAPTER 10

Good Governance

Establishing Commitment

Committing to a set of ethics and basing your decisions and actions on these needs, above all, trust. It needs trust in the senior management that they will see actions and any mistakes in the proper context and that regulators will also trust good intent and sound crucible process. Making and using crucibles is essentially a collective experience. Maturity is not necessarily IQ dependent, it does not need or feed circles of exclusivity and power, and in its best form, it does not need acceding, rights, or accreditation. It is open to robust challenge and debate—it is about giving room to form good judgments. Good process is never a substitute for good judgment.

While there are many contributory factors to developing "commitment," the focus of this book is on corporate maturity and authenticity so we will consider here only those aspects of governance and leadership that contribute to moving an organizational system from being simply effective to exhibiting the attributes of maturity.

While so much of governance must rest on the quality of systems and controls, especially the efficacy and voracity of information gathering, recording, and reporting, and the subsequent communication, dissemination, and monitoring of decisions, the differential that distinguishes adequate, even successful governance from a mature system is the essential qualities of the decision making and evaluation that sits at the very heart of the entire governance construction.

Commitment is assisted by three key aspects:

1. The integrity of the decision-making process
2. Real independence
3. Dealing with complexity

We will consider these three in detail:

Before addressing these we should note the clearest expression of the core importance of ethics to a company—and the board's role in setting and steering ethics—is set out in the Higgs Code, an early contributor code to the UK's Corporate Governance Code.* Higgs states:

> *The Board is collectively responsible for promoting the success of the company by directing and supervising the company's affairs. The Board's role is to provide entrepreneurial leadership of the company within a framework of prudent and effective controls that enable risk to be assessed and managed. The Board should set the company's strategic aims, ensure that the necessary financial and human resources are in place for the company to meet its objectives, and review management performance. The Board should set the company's values and standards and ensure* that its obligations to its shareholders and others are understood and met.

Decision-Making Structures

This basic structure (Figure 10.1) suggests a way of making more mature judgments:

Good governance needs more constructive challenge processes—opportunities and structures for thought, debate, and challenge. These should be built into everyday situations and processes, in business, in public life, in communities, in education, that explicitly and directly encourage individual and collective questioning and quality deliberation.

Challenge processes are frameworks (of processes or regulations for companies, maybe) that both allow challenge to occur in a nonunusual, depersonalized (sometimes), and reasonable way and provide a structure for that questioning that is flexible but also enabling and organized. They give permission for questions to be raised that might not otherwise be brought forward without fear of embarrassment, detriment, or awkwardness. And they are built up from principles and values that the group finds both important and useful.

---

* *From the Higgs Report 2002*

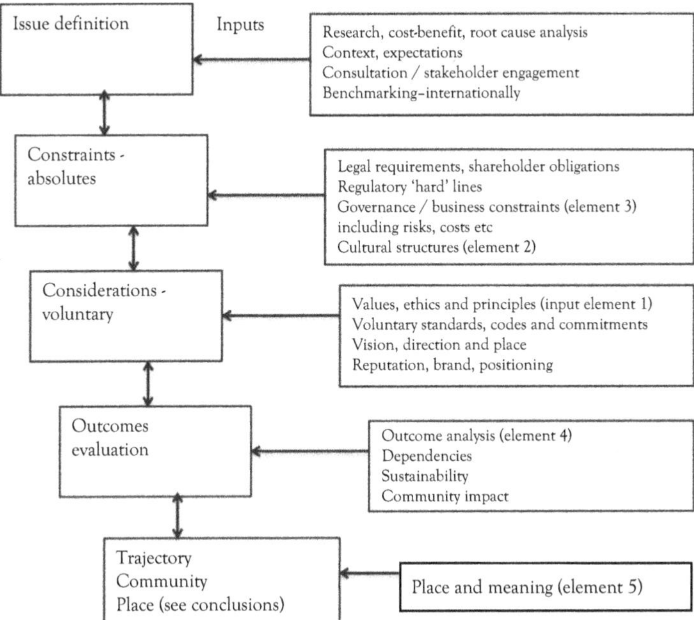

Figure 10.1 Decision-making structure

It is crucial that such principles are neither ideologically driven, we are not suggesting a simply moralistic position, nor purely a business case. The key is complexity. Challenge process questions bring together the long term and short, the individual and collective perspective, the outcomes and good process, the transcendent and the visceral.

It is not about precooked solutions, we have no agenda here, or even worse the political operating system of "nudge"—which would appear in a challenge process as deceitful and corrosive. This is about opening debate to all and empowering absolutely everyone in everyday situations, making decisions, dealing with a complaint, setting a strategy, mending a problem where there are no rules, starting a community club, being a good neighbor. It goes far beyond any notion of community.

The value of a challenge process lies in not just identifying the historical influences on one's own practice but also acknowledging that this practice is in itself an influence and that one has a responsibility to one's self, peers, organization, society, and now increasingly the environment. It is identifying and either confirming or reforming the balances and counterbalances of these influences that these challenge processes are all about and perhaps considering the following themes.

Constructive Challenge

But quite often one question or set of questions is not enough, we need a series of questions that are seen in combination and interact. They may be specially devised and selected for the circumstances of a particular organization and may evolve over time as the level of maturity develops.

The following *questions* are designed to help recognize, apply, and balance ethics and values in everyday decisions and actions. They are grouped around the core ethics identified earlier.

Structured constructive challenge.

Open, Honest, Responsive, and Accountable

- Who is left out or kept in the dark? Why?
- How happy are we to be associated with our decisions or actions?
- Are we listening or just hearing?
- What can we learn? How do we help others to understand us?
- How do we recognize and deal with conflicts of interest?

Relating to Colleagues and Customers Fairly and with Respect

- Do we treat everyone as we would like to be treated?
- Do we deal with people with respect and without prejudice?
- How do we keep rights and obligations in balance and proportionate?
- When do we hold to our commitments and resist "fudging"?
- Who benefits and who loses out? Should they?

Committed to Acting Competently, Responsibly, and Reliably

- Do we do what we say we will do?
- Under pressure do we swap cooperation for coercion?
- Do we dither or delay? How is error treated?

- Do people trust us? If not, why not?
- Can we meet our commitments and plans?

To embed these values the following is needed:

Developing Vision and a Values-Led Approach

- What needs changing? What prevents change?
- What is the long-term outcome? What is sustainable?
- Do we sufficiently recognize and act on our stakeholder responsibilities?
- How do we develop shared purpose, loyalty, and fulfillment?
- Do we apply ethical criteria simply to gain an advantage or because we believe we should?

Conflicts and tensions can arise in using constructive challenge for a number of different reasons:

- The pressure of short-term gain could be seen to encourage undesirable behavior. Staff bonus payments may often seem to be geared to pure bottom-line success. How risks and tensions can be identified is a constant issue—e.g., truth versus loyalty, one person versus the many? In all of this it is usual for the values and actions of senior management to influence employee levels.
- Some individuals behave unethically because they think it is worth the risk. This may be related to a short-termism agenda, or may be simply personally selfish. People weigh up the pros and cons and take a chance. It is a deliberate risk or reward trade off.
- Others may believe they are behaving ethically but come to operate by a different yardstick to that used by others. They might do something which is deemed unethical, but which seems acceptable from their own perspective.
- Some (and some of these groups are not mutually exclusive) may be unaware of the values embedded in existing regulatory

standards. So, they comply (or not) blindly with the "letter of the law," rather than thinking about the wider effects their behavior might have.

The Importance of Independent Judgment

Who'd be a nonexecutive director (NED)? A good NED often makes a material difference to the value of a business and steering the shareholder and regulatory relationships into a positive direction. But the responsibilities of NEDs are significant in bringing forward a culture of maturity that is, for a business to develop a "culture of accountability" at all levels and for senior individuals to be fully accountable for defined business activities and material risks, build public confidence and improve the outcomes for consumers and the wider community.

Some key NED responsibilities[†]:

1. Scrutinizing the performance of management in meeting agreed goals and objectives
2. Monitoring the reporting of performance
3. Satisfying themselves on the integrity of financial information
4. Satisfying themselves that financial controls and systems of risk management are robust and defensible
5. Scrutinizing the design and implementation of the remuneration policy
6. Providing objective views on resources, appointments, and standards of conduct
7. Being involved in succession planning

These are all vital to provide effective independent challenge, voting where necessary, and the NEDs need to keep themselves sufficiently informed and skilled to perform these roles. NEDs are not (and should not be) executive and so cannot be held to the same level of accountability but nevertheless they are equally involved and bound by collective board decision making—indeed that is the point.

† FCA COCON Annex in CP 17–25.

NEDs should be leaders, having the time and perspective necessary to see the purpose and ensure the integrity. They should, for example, insist on defining responsibilities for all senior staff and committees clearly and explore what it means to have duties of care, to build the new closer relationships, and to review the positions from which we make judgments.

The value of independent judgment is that it brings a selfless and disinterested point of view to the business process that is new and distinctive. If independent input is only to rubberstamp someone else's decision, usually from the line, then really as a function and adds very little value and may rightly be held in low esteem.

But this perspective is not just about interpreting what regulator says, which has been the traditional safe position of compliance, but rather setting any interpretation within a broader context of wider standards and practices and adding a range of opinions options drawn from experience about what is practical and maybe achievable. An independent needs to bring to bear an understanding of overseas best practices, an absorption of learning from relevant enforcement cases, regulatory speeches, guidance, peer group sharing, and information from many other formal and informal sources.

Dealing with Complexity

It is clear from the preceding that preserving independence does not mean that decision making is any easier. In fact, it is hard to overemphasize the inherently complicated nature of businesses and organization yet still we are so often drawn to shortcuts and quick fixes, that while understandably highly attractive, only serve to undermine maturity of good governance. It's not just ticking boxes that we need to leave behind, it's the widespread conception in business that there is an easy answer to be had and a cheap, off-the-shelf, plug-in and play solution always available. How boards think that simple decision trees or risk maps will provide a credible answer, or that culture can be "fixed" by a one-hour annual training is quite extraordinary. Scenarios and stress tests need to be worked through in real time, various competing options calibrated in different ways, a wide range of regulatory or nonregulatory sources referenced, and logical, structured, constructive challenge, and debate carried through at every level. It goes without saying that verifying the validity of information and voracity of conventional board dashboards and audit management information is so important in this age characterized by "fake news" and "alternative facts." Shedding light on a "grey area" or conflict-of-interest, or balancing competing priorities is a tall order and requires a disciplined, intellectual approach and practical methodologies (of which businesses rarely have sufficient that they have home grown). Many judgments are indeed fine judgments or such close calls that it is the absolute core skill of good governance to dissect these delicate threads and weave a realistic and durable solution—and then to sell it to others and monitor its introduction.

So the complexity agenda is helped by:

- Finding more suitable and relevant sources of information
- Weighing up their usefulness in the light of practical experience, benchmarking, or published guidance
- Applying new ideas in a structured and disciplined way
- Identifying and testing "deciding principles"
- Making others aware of the decision-making process used
- Building in methods of real-time monitoring to evaluate success
- Finding new ways of calibration and evaluation
- Devising tools to assist the decision-making process

Triangulation

This is a useful conceptual tool critical to the quality of complex decision making and to maturity.

There is usually no such thing in organizations as a pure ethical question or a solely "ethical dilemma" or a numbers issue. Even though there may be many tools or decision-making exercises or training courses or even ethics exams, these are all far too abstract from the pressures and situations of everyday situations.

It is always necessary to find a way of weighing up and bringing together influences and information from many sources. You need to bring into play as many sources of reference as possible.

- Rulebooks
- Precedents
- Standards from other sectors or international bodies
- Regulatory speeches and statements
- Recorded conversations with regulators
- Correspondence with regulators

These give bearings toward finding an acceptable ethical position in a method that resembles "triangulation" used in map-making and in-route finding, that is, working from at least two "known" points to provide a basis for deciding where you could be located (See Figure 10.2).

Figure 10.2 Triangulation

This process of triangulation provides an "area" in which it is safe and ethical for the firm to operate and it can choose a number of different positions if it wishes to differentiate its ethical position slightly. The more reference points the better.

It is pressured complex moments that both test and demonstrate organizations accumulated experience, the depth of their learning and practiced powers of their judgment. These are the marks of a true maturity.

CHAPTER 11

Sustainable Outcomes and Community

What is the impact of decisions and actions, and on whom?

Why Is Outcome So Important?

Outcome changes everything. Outcome is a perspective that looks from the other end of the telescope, not focusing on internal processes and culture (behavior) nor indeed on outputs, but on the impacts of decisions, actions, and behaviors on others outside the organization and the long-term "life" consequences for them. These outcomes are more than customer experience or satisfaction. Outcome is more important than whether the customer was "happy" with the service they received (a relatively superficial matter, often measured by customer satisfaction surveys) or even whether they would recommend the company (typically measured by a net promoter score). Indeed the outcome will emerge for many years, which is part of the problem of measuring the full consequences. Equally, a positive outcome may be more than just avoiding detriment (the minimum level that has traditionally provided a benchmark for regulation), but may be the choice between a wide range of upside options where the real test is measuring the "most right" choice, or avoiding the loss of opportunities for the customer and their dependents; such as housing options, leisure and lifestyle choices, school choices, employment opportunities, and so on (i.e., opportunity costs). Outcomes, where measurable, feedback to shape the organization's of view of ethics, culture and good governance. A mature organization requires a strong grasp of implications of outcome and requires some form of outcome evaluation.

This is not to say that prior emphases on ethics, culture, and governance is less important, but outcome adds a new layer to the "cake" that can override other considerations and it thus provides a challenge or measuring stick against which to judge the contribution of the earlier elements.

So it is not that processes and internal controls suddenly fail to matter, but they do not constitute *all* that matters in a mature organization—and very obviously not. Consequently, for example, it is not a tenable excuse or defense to say that any one decision or action is appropriate is because the organization is simply following good process and making the necessary declarations and reporting transparently - if the ultimate impacts are not positive, or the most positive that are possible in the circumstances. Of course, this raises the question of what is *positive*. A yardstick for *positive outcome* emerges in the final section of this chapter.

In a customer service generation we are often fixated by the quality of service test. It is not enough to "be customer friendly"; organizations also have to deliver desirable, suitable results for the consumer. A telephone call maybe answered efficiently and rapidly (which normally equals good customer service) and in a friendly manner (which suggests a contribution to a satisfactory customer experience) but the outcome of the product may still be in some way damaging or less than positive. We must be clear to differentiate outcome from other similar and related terms (Figure 11.1).

Deciding what a "positive" result will be will vary between specific sets of circumstances and sectors norms and types of customers, and depends greatly on the context and even the time horizon over which an outcome is (or can be) evaluated. What may be considered a positive outcome in the short term (such as a decent sale price or low fees) may well not

Service levels	Customer experience	TCF	**Outcomes**
Calls answered per hour	Call response time 'One-touch'	Fair resolution in timescale	Good result in terms of life outcomes / expectations
Sales targets met	Clear, no small print courteous	True, fair and not mis-leading	Low barriers to entry and exit no 'fat profit'
% market share increased	Choice of product options	Fair dealing wake up packs.	Services for excluded
Complaints down	Attractive rates follows complaint handling rules	Root cause less legalize	Write-off for vulnerable

Figure 11.1 What is and is not outcome

Note: TCF = Treating Customers Fairly, is a common standard for customer focused culture.

pass muster years later (when the product or service fails to deliver the expected results or customers discover that the switching or exit charges are disproportionately high), or vice versa. The organization needs to decide in its own context what amounts to a "positive or desirable results."

Consequently, outcome evaluation and subsequent measurement is not just a matter of mechanics, but a more subtle and evaluation, weighing up positives and negatives for the different types of customer over a variety of time horizons. It may be argued that outcome can only be measured individually for each customer, but to be effective outcome needs to be considered in terms of general principles and categories of customer type. This evaluation will be a continuous process of checking what exactly has transpired and how impacts become cumulative and how the various outcomes interact with each other. Aggregated outcome is likely to become a new feature of overall risk management.

Outcome Issues

First, outcome is part of conduct risk and encompasses all the effects of an organization's actions and inactions, behaviors, statements, positions, and influences. These effects may be specific or general, immediate or long term. They may be collective or discrete and firms in the same sector operating similarly may create systemic outcomes. These, in turn, may be local, national, or international. The scales are infinitely varied.

Second, who is the impact upon? In this context, the primary focus for most businesses will be on consumers and potential consumers, but in fact increasingly regulatory concern runs to the wider impacts on the economy and society including those who may not be your customers. They may be dependents, children, older people, relatives, friends, associates, colleagues, and so on. The impact may be more diffuse such as effects on general levels of confidence, investment, spending, and saving.

Third, there needs to be an extensive process of stakeholder identification for any firm to do to understand who its stakeholders are and their interests. This process has little meaning unless it is continuous and involves two-way communication and engagement, especially so that stakeholders can understand and become educated about a firm's operating model, intentions, planned impacts, and prospects. Stakeholders need to be ranked by the materiality of their interest.

The types of impacts that might be considered include:

1. The accessibility to products and services at that price point, especially for first time consumers;
2. The contribution made to helping start-ups or small businesses;
3. The number of options, allowing for choice, competition, and flexibility, the ease of switching, fair return, and security;
4. Extra help or consideration for low-paid and vulnerable, those in short- and long-term difficulty or debt;
5. Access for those who find themselves or chose to be in some way excluded from that market place;
6. Ways of helping special categories such as servicemen, students, and job seekers; and
7. Impacts on levels of confidence and trust in the industry as a whole.

Fourth, all of these considerations have complicated and even unintended consequences. To take just one example, helping a customer to manage his or her debt through a debt management plan in the shortest possible time sounds like positive outcome. However, if the criterion is the shortest possible time, then it is likely that a high proportion of the customer's disposable income will be absorbed in the scheme leaving a potentially low quality of life for the customer and their family and potentially a residual level of resentment, which may conceivably lead to a "binge" of overspending immediately after the plan is concluded. Is it not better that lesser payments are demanded over a longer period of time so that the customer can have the chance to learn financial management and prudent planning so that they didn't return to previously high spending ways and fall back into debt. Is this not a better long-term outcome for the customer and wider society?

Managing Outcome

Organizational outcomes are affected by a wide range of internal policy choices, such as:

1. The willingness to cross subsidize new customers from existing customers;

2. The construction of scoring systems to exclude certain groups;
3. The use of targets to control or encourage aggressive selling;
4. Attitudes toward vulnerable consumers;
5. The use of teaser rates or lost leaders to encourage new business;
6. Readiness to offer forbearance to nonpayers, or ensure debt collection;
7. Striking an appropriate balance of benefits between organizations and customer; and
8. The level of investment in ensuring the competence of staff.

The list is, of course, infinite. That is why maturity is developed in the process of deciding what constitutes and develops positive outcomes.

An outcome-based approach may free an organization from producing nonstandard innovative solutions escaping from standardized or benchmarked processes and systems. With the focus on outcome, companies can tailor their offerings in a much more individual way. Management has freedom in:

1. Determining the new kinds of offering that can be made, within the boundaries of relevant principles;
2. Evaluating and monitoring the short, medium, and long-term impact on various customer groups in their own terms;
3. Changing the focus of monitoring from process to outcome contributes crucially to the viability of new kinds of product, how advice is offered and how charges, terms, and conditions and policies are applied;
4. Allowing compliance to explore new and innovative methods of product design and monitoring that contribute directly to competitive advantage;
5. Provide direct inputs to determining regulatory criteria and priorities.

Measurement of Outcomes

There is no commonly agreed framework as yet for the evaluation of outcomes across many sectors; that is, what principles could reasonably be included and how these principles might be measured, in isolation or in combination, on a consistent basis.

The lack of such a common framework, it is suggested, makes the development of the important outcome perspective less effective and more problematic for both organizations and regulatory bodies. Without at least a description of the *dimensions* of outcome it is more difficult for organizations to mature and it also has an indirect effect on maturity, as it is difficult to comply with emerging standards, thus leaving organizations that do not understand outcome vulnerable to what might appear to be subjective regulatory judgments and potentially uncontrolled sanctions. It is more difficult for regulators to establish or embed a common platform across a sector of outcomes and encourage the kinds of improvements it wishes to see. It is not desirable or practical for regulators to become overly specific, as this would add yet another layer of prescriptive regulation sector and internationally.* However, organizations may vary from devising elaborate and comprehensive measures of outcome which shape all their processes and compliance, while other organizations do not understand the difference between consumer outcome and consumer experience or customer service.

A suitable framework could set out:

1. The elements of consumer outcome that could or should be considered;
2. Illustrations of how these apply to major product areas;
3. Suitable practical metrics for assessing each element;
4. An indication of how to evaluate, using these metrics, whether an outcome is positive or negative; and
5. A system for ongoing review and updating as economic and demographic situations change.

This might take the form of a matrix of consumer outcome elements against product type, with the desirable metrics in each cell (see Table 11.1):

Importantly, the elements outcome will not just be financial advantage and disadvantage, but also impacts on quality-of-life, access to

* Jackman, D. 2015. *The Compliance Revolution: How Compliance Needs to Change to Survive*. Singapore: John Wiley & Sons.

Table 11.1 An outcomes maturity matrix

Product or service	Key issues	Outcomes from minimal compliance regime	Outcomes from conservative tick box compliance	Outcomes from business-led compliance	Outcomes from a confident values-led culture
Mortgages	Access to lending for vulnerable groups and commitment under pressure	Basic products; low persistency dislocation in housing market repossession aggressive	Only “safe” customers eligible on points system; disempowerment of community Homelessness or parents home	Tailored products, wider range, competitive rates, greater choice and flexibility	Customer needs met, even when nonstandard, same offer to existing customers, ethical options
Insurance	Premiums not prohibitive, reasonable conditions, effective competition	Targeting high margin, Poor service and follow-up, price “following”	Tick box approval, web supermarkets, “Hidden” exclusions in small print	Marginal markets tailored to specific hard-to-meet needs e.g., health	Flexible payments, periods, and so on. No small print Open conditions
Deposits	Range of services, security, rates	Limited number of standard accounts	High level of Know Your Customer (KYC) Low interest Inflexible	More creative rates and services	Something different: in services, charging, access
Credit cards	Flexibility of payment, charging, access	…			

opportunities (employment, education, leisure), life-chances, affects on all forms of health, consumer education and capability, the overall balance of individual risk and resilience, a swell as long- and short-term economic impacts; and since the financial services affect all aspects of life, conceivably proxy measures of happiness, well-being, and fulfillment.

As a first step, boards and other management levels may consider the following action checklist to at least make inroads into capturing and managing outcome.

Actions

A useful check for management and a board could be the following questions:

1. How have you designed your governance structures and processes to ensure that consumer outcomes are central to your strategy and decision making?
2. How are you ensuring that decisions consider all material stakeholders and are fairly taken?
3. How do you ensure no one stakeholder has an unfair outcome or degree of influence in determining outcomes?
4. How do you encourage the free flow of ideas, contributions, and information into the outcome-centered compliance?
5. How easily can any relevant interested parties find outcome statements and evaluations and how can they feedback?
6. How do you reduce barriers to progress and bureaucracy to allow innovation, appropriate risk, diversity, and prosperity?
7. How do you consciously develop a mindset that values the outcomes for all sections of the community, vulnerable customers and those generations that follow us?
8. Do you measure realistic and practical outcome expectations?

Community Outcomes

If it is not possible to define industry specific outcomes in terms of customer impacts, the next stage is to consider aggregated impacts (the combination of many individual decisions) on the wider community and society. We will call these community outcomes, and in this area there is greater definition and progress.

The aggregate effect of many individual outcomes may well have impacts on the effective functioning and cohesiveness of entire communities, or create differential effects that open opportunities for some groups and reduce the opportunities for others. This may lead to differential impacts by geographic area, or by social group or by demographics and thereby have implications for social cohesion, integration, and identity. Determining positive or desirable outcome, therefore, has wider implications for any mature and responsible organization acting as any good citizen would. The broad architecture may well be internationally or politically determined, but the finer detail at least needs to be assessed by the industry sector organizations and their relevant regulators together.

What Is Community?

Community arises from the normal human interaction of a group of people working, living, or interacting together who often share or develop common interests, values, and identity. They may associate their community with a "sense of place" or feel they belong to a dispersed or virtual community. The degree of cohesiveness may change over time as relationships deepen and mature or weaken, but in general the ties that bring people together outweigh the differences. Communities often find the need to develop organizing principles, systems, and structures from within (grassroots initiatives) or forms of administration may be imposed "top-down" by wider society that shape and define the development of the community.

The Importance of Community

Community can be considered the ultimate point of reference for a company or a sector; it provides definition for its role and justification for its existence. If community needs and expectations change, the sector must reflect these changing needs or the companies will lose their legitimacy and fail to be supported and patronized. Companies can also help to shape communities' perceptions of needs through marketing, while consumers also feedback through their choices.

However, community ultimately determines the services that are necessary and the patterns of behavior from organizations that are acceptable. Community exercises control through:

- Providing the legitimacy to carry out business through issuing a license to practice by regulatory or governmental authorities, reflecting the communities will or interests.
- Consumer purchasing decisions—community members will not, ideally, purchase products and services that are injurious to the wider purposes or the community, financial services being a service function.
- Investment decisions—communities will, through direct public and indirect private investment choices, select to invest in those vehicles that best suit broader aims.

The Role of Companies in Community

The purpose of a company is much more complex than shareholder return. Companies play a role in the wider society and economy by doing something. They add value by creating and consuming a wide range of products or materials, manufacturing, servicing, collecting and distributing, trading, entertaining, educating, or building for the future. They buy from and support a ring of suppliers, large and small. There is in effect an outcome or series of outcomes, all of which have some use, meaning, or worth. Very few companies could get away with producing something nobody needs or values.

The role companies play goes further, to providing employment which in turn generates salaries and benefits for families, which in turn again allows for purchasing from local stores, producers, and thereby supports a penumbra of other businesses, their employees, and families. Employment also gives individuals and their families benefits in terms of a sense of identity, worth, and confidence; it provides economic and social stability, and by creating environments and architectures companies shape the built fabric and natural landscape around us. This is both a contribution in the present and a heritage for the future.

Companies are hubs for local communities, generators of wealth—which is fed into the local economy—as well as part of the social fabric; a focus for meeting, exchanging ideas, innovation, participation, and sometimes even celebration. Companies create activity, pay taxes and rates, affect local democracy and contribute to local causes. They are part of the scenery, the sense of place. Companies, whether they are aware of it or not, have a purpose in playing a part as corporate citizens, with at least the same responsibilities as individuals. This line of reasoning may not resonate with some companies, but it needs to so they can start to define their purpose beyond pure monetary profit.

This is a very solid purpose and role and brings with it a sense of identity and real responsibilities. If a company decides to streamline a process and therefore make a number of employees redundant, that decision has a spiral of effect on local wealth, businesses, families, services, and future prospects. Its purpose has in some respects been damaged, but companies rarely see it in that way. Some would say all of this is too complicated—but reality is complicated and the effects of company actions can be just as significant as policy changes by government, or at least local government, and such changes would be open to a high level of public scrutiny and debate, as well as accountability. No one would reasonably expect such detailed debate for a normal company decision, unless they were a state concern or involved in a strategic project such as building a new airport, power station, or railway line where the planning process would allow for public engagement. Yet how can companies exercise some level of awareness and engagement about purpose and responsibility while still working effectively?

Engaging in the Community Dimension

There is a strong impetus to take this area seriously. We may suggest that those services and firms that are sustainable and best adjusted to community aims will survive and prosper, while those ill adjusted will not.

So it is important to understand the fundamental interests and purposes of community. Naturally, there will be variations in detail but is possible to elucidate general areas of community interest as a starting point (Table 11.2).

Table 11.2 Purposes of community

Purpose of sustainability	Examples
Attractiveness	Appeal to citizens and other interested parties, for example, investors; belonging; culture; place; sense of identity
Preservation and improvement of environment	Improved environmental performance, including reducing greenhouse gas emissions; protection, restoration and enhancement of biological diversity and ecosystem services, including protection of ecosystems, plant and animal diversity, and migration as well as genetic diversity; reduced health hazard
Resilience	Anticipation; climate change mitigation and adaptation; economic shocks and stresses preparedness, social evolution
Responsible resource use	Consumption; distribution; improved land management; reducing, reusing and recycling of materials; respect for scarcity of all types of resources (natural, human, financial); sustainable production, storage, and transport
Social cohesion	Accessibility; culture; dialogue with external parties not limited by boundaries, diversity; equity; heritage; inclusiveness; inequalities reduction; rootedness; sense of belonging; and social mobility
Well-being	Access to opportunities; creativity, education; happiness; healthy environment; human capital improvement; livable city; prosperity; quality of life; security; self-confidence; welfare

Some of these concepts need further explanation:

- Mutuality—better able to act for shared or common benefit.
- Connectedness and sense of place—rootedness in a distinctive locale. Shared experiences and cultural traditions, sense of identity, belonging.
- Intracommunity equity—equity between and within different groups, diversity, inclusiveness, social mobility, and unconditionality.
- Intergenerational equity—equity between people alive today and future generations, equal access to opportunities; education; happiness; healthy environment.
- Building capability—investing in human capital improvement.
- Custodianship—responsible use of shared resources and the environment.

- Prosperous, resilient, and adaptable—capable of creating wealth and bouncing back from adverse situations and respond to the changing circumstances, seeking opportunities, taking risks. Investing in social capital and the power to create, prosperity, quality of life, celebration; security, welfare.
- Shared external relationships—open to outside ideas, people, and contributions integrating new and existing links and traditions, not limited by boundaries.

How does this translate into organizations' understanding? The following Table 11.3 gives some illustrations:

Table 11.3 Community outcomes in practice

Mutuality is derived from the fact that a group of people, through cooperation, are better able to act for their mutual benefit than if acting alone. From this simple but central tenet, comes the overarching objective of mutuality: namely, that mutuals seek to benefit their members' quality of life rather than maximize profit.	Respect for all members in the community, where irrespective of age, background–physical and social mobility–all are considered and treated with dignity and given the chance to belong and participate. Collective grassroots initiatives, for example, cooperatives such as housing associations and credit unions.
Engagement, inclusivity, and accountability—inclusive participation based on strong democratic principles and good governance—differences are encouraged but are mediated and are resolvable. Accountability to the wider community legitimizes empowerment and capacity building to help the community develop confidence and capability.	Distinctive contribution—individuals or groups bring particular contribution to the table on the basis of pooled responsibility and resources. Principled localism—neighborhood solutions within shared vision and principles e.g., early years incubators, local sourcing, collective use of community space.
Connectedness and sense of place—understanding the close interaction between economic, social, and environment aspects within a locale. Shared experiences and appreciating what is distinctive and special about the local area, including landscape, biodiversity, architecture, and heritage. Cultural traditions in the area are also important in giving and defining an area's character.	Empathy and understanding of others' needs and aspirations, limitations. Coherence of identity (overlapping social and economic interactions). Strengthening and promotion of local identity through mutuality and reciprocity. Using local schools, shops, working near-to-home, mutually supportive neighbors, street markets, shared housing ownership schemes.

Intracommunity equity is the principle of equity between and within different communities and groups. It implies that consumption and production in one community should not undermine the ecological, social, and economic basis for other communities to maintain or improve their quality of life.	Providing affordable housing, diversity of employment, flexible and inclusive service design which meets the needs of all consumers, regardless of their abilities. Reinforcing health and individual and community well-being.
Intergenerational equity is the principle of equity between people alive today and future generations. Unsustainable production and consumption by today's society could degrade the ecological, social, and economic basis for tomorrow's society, whereas community sustainability involves ensuring that future generations will have the means to achieve a quality of life equal to or better than that of today.	Planning for the long-term vision not just short-term gain or "fix." Environmental stewardship schemes. Use of renewable energy. Land and building reuse. Designing homes and spaces for "lifetime" needs reducing the need to move. Cohousing—intergenerational, young, and old mutually supporting each other.
Prosperous, resilient, and adaptable—communities are capable of creating wealth and bouncing back from adverse situations and respond to the changing circumstances. Not only protecting against risks but also making seeking opportunities. Investing in social capital. Know-how and skills that is shared within and across neighborhoods.	Cooperative investment, diverse training, premium support for skills, and job opportunities. For those unable to gain paid work, being meaningfully engaged in neighborhood. Community capability and competence audits. Collective values are shared through community education and representational empowerment.
Shared external relationships—open to outside ideas, people, and contributions.	Care for connected communities. Play part in wider community as leader or beacon.

Table 11.4 Constructive challenge questions relating to community outcomes

To what extent do policies and strategies businesses deploy in communities contribute to expanding, maintaining, or eroding their sense of community shared identity? How do the cultural policies in communities contribute to their attractiveness?
To what extent is the natural environment a source of inspiration for identity and values in communities and does the business recognize and enhance the environment?
Are changes in culture and identity expected in the local community? If so how can the business anticipate and help or slow the transition; why will change happen and when?
How is community culture a useful indicator of business success?
How does the business enable greater accessibility and affordability to cultural events in communities?
What does business contribute to developing a distinct sense of community identity, individually or collectively?

These interests can be related back to the governance questions developed under constructive challenge and the following (Tables 11.4 and 11.5) are question sets that may be introduced into the constructive challenge to help address the community dimension:

Evaluating Community Outcome

Progress is being made on what constitutes community maturity in the International Standards Organization's (ISO) work on sustainable, resilient, and smart communities and cities—the ISO 37101 series first published in 2016. This provides the framework against which organizations can start to measure their positive contribution to community outcomes.

Corporate maturity at the level of a community is presented in the form of a maturity matrix. An extract of a draft version (prepared by the author for the UK contribution to ISO 37101) is included in the following and a full version is available from ISO or national standards organizations:

The Role of Businesses

A debate started in 2009 about the "social usefulness" of business and their role in community.[†] This was a genuine question about the community outcomes following the financial crash, which was, and still is, greatly misunderstood and these questions have broadened out to cover the role of capitalism. What may have been useful at the time was a discussion about the role society and communities want businesses to perform and the social and economic "goods" or outcomes we can trust them to deliver.

The rational part of the discussion ran into the sand as it was too soon after the crises of 2008 but has been revived many times since. In particular, it has translated into some highly impactful legislation such as the climate change treaties, energy price caps, senior management and certification regime (SM&CR), and policies aimed at "ring fencing" certain services—such as putting in place a distinction between retail and wholesale banking. That discussion will result in retail banks having to adopt the role of utilities

---

[†] Turner, A. September 22, 2009. *Speech by Chairman, FSA at the City Banquet.* London: The Mansion House.

Table 11.5 Maturity matrix for communities

	Start-up	Establishing coherent framework	Integration and embedding	Leadership and innovation
Mutuality	Community-wide approach that consciously and creatively, in a planned way, seeks to make the area or community more attractive to external parties (e.g., inward investors) and to community. Initial community meetings or surveys to identify local issues. Competence mapping of community skills and resources. Basic initiatives to demonstrate and *enhance shared benefits of mutual working and sustainability*. Building sense of belonging; culture; place; and identity e.g., through using local architecture and materials, produce.	Coordinated and structured funding applications for sustainability projects or tax or rate advantages negotiated for brownfield sites. Community external promotion—materials, websites, signage, campaigns. Basic needs such as security may need to be dealt with before other progress can be made.	Create new transport infrastructure to attract inward investment. Energy diversification schemes that deliver city-wide balanced resources at attractive rates.	Build capacity for long term for wider community i.e., shared learning. Extend scope and export skills to other communities where needs e.g., International beacon ISO 37101 pilot city.

Social Cohesion	Activities and structures that bring meaning and sense of collective journey, shared experiences, common risks and opportunities, shared values and interests, responsibilities, and commitment to the community and belonging. Welcoming to all members of the community and new comers and outsiders: community forum or website, public space use, celebrations, sports events that draw on local heritage and culture and traditions. Common kindness and caring for weaker members of the community in need.	Focus on reduction of inequities and increasing social integration. Focus on opening accessibility to jobs, housing, opportunities, information, positions, and so on. Local planning or internal corporate or local government purchasing rules to require (%) use of local suppliers and employees. Local occupancy clauses for sustainable and affordable housing.	Engagement of marginalized members of community offering support to vulnerable members such as food banks, refugee assistance, language training, financial support, benefits eligibility identification, housing support. Conscious corporate and government procedures for positive encouragement of diversity, protection of rights, and public transparency of diversity levels.	Community defined by what holds it together rather the boundaries that divide from others. Open to ideas, dialogue or exchange, and influences. Multi-community networks, co-working facilities, flexible child care, shared transport schemes. Creativity and artistic expression can have a powerful affect on building community identity and cohesion.

Well-being	Well-being as a strong focus for the awareness of issues and starter schemes, e.g., keep fit schemes, evening education classes, and litter reduction. Identify less obvious needs, e.g., stress and mental health needs, the creative use of public space and diversity of employment and housing opportunities and education.	Avoid simple, tick box methods of identifying and measuring well-being; communities are complex and require composite measures of well-being, often including qualitative elements such as quality of life, happiness, or satisfaction. Cross-issue schemes to deal with several well-being issues at once e.g., business training or school partnerships, safety in design and neighborhood crime-watch. One difficulty is the unknown risks emerging and the unintended consequences of new initiatives.	Community engages in longer term and more fundamental, radical change as self-confidence and experience builds, which may involve some costs for greater benefits, e.g., multiple use of public assets such as public halls and schools and flexible work- house or co-housing. Embed sustainable development purposes through local government policies, planning, and tax and rent controls.	Community explicitly recognized, managed and evaluated as a human capital. Well-being understood in deeper and more complex ways as expectations change, incorporating the diversity and evolving nature of all generations. Community promotion of well being and sustainable development. Influence on wider agendas. Inward investment "factors in" well-being value(s) and commit to extend and build capacity and engagement.

and adopting a very different set of behaviors and strategies than in the past without the consequent rewards.

A range of studies, including the Stieglitz report on "Gross National Happiness"—as an alternative to Gross National Product (GNP)—have informed an even wider debate on the forms of progress that society should consider and the appropriate role for business. These alternative measures of wealth reflect individual awareness of "well-being" and an increased weighing of ethical issues. This determines what we want to see from retailers and suppliers, including financial services suppliers. This trend may simply be a luxury, an expression of an affluent middle class, living longer. But changing attitudes affect behavior and choices. We may decide to tone down our aspirations and work rate in favor of less tangible but more fulfilling ways of spending our time.

The largest global corporations can have more influence than some individual nation states, and their globalized nature can elevate them above and beyond the reach of national regulators and tax authorities. We have seen concerns about Google, Starbucks, and Amazon not paying what appear to be unreasonable levels of tax in the countries in which they generate their profitability. The UK chancellor announced in December 2014 measures to close loopholes on accounting practices that allow profits to be diffused. The so-called "Google tax" has also been proposed in recognition of the growing public disquiet about corporate behavior and the attitudes and values they reveal. Some consumers may cease patronizing certain retailers and products. A foretaste of the power of consumer views about community issues was the boycotting of cheap tee-shirts from high street stores following the appalling loss of life in Bangladesh when a clothing factory, known to be unsafe, collapsed killing many workers on low pay. Retailers have sought to find new suppliers and issue declarations of good practice in relation to their supply chains and workers' conditions—community legitimacy is beginning to bite.

Conclusions

Boards need to understand the organization's role in its own wider community. This is vital for the organization's sustainability and the prosperity of the community.

> The key to unraveling this disjuncture lies with the values of businesses, how they are applied—or not—in decision making and the place of companies in the wider community companies too often appear to operate in a bubble, detached from everyday lives precisely because there does not seem to be a connection between corporate aims and those of the wider community. The Companies Act requirements, forged in a very different age, appear to provide cover for the single-minded pursuit of bottom-line performance and shareholder value (in a period of intense Victorian expansion when it was necessary to provide investors some protection in environments of extreme unknowable risk such as overseas ventures e.g., railways etc.).
>
> We should be saying "just grow up" …

The solution lies in a number of steps that explicitly focus on building a corporate maturity and bridging a connection between corporate aims and broader social objectives.[‡]

Community is the ultimate point of reference for a company or a sector; it provides definition for its role and justification for its existence. The sustainable path or place of equilibrium is an industry in balance with its community. An industry which is providing more or less the services and products expected and needed by the community, enabling it to achieve its objectives, to prosper and provide sustainable wealth and well-being to all its members fairly.

The purpose of a company and the meaning of work are much more complex than shareholder return. Companies play a role in the wider society and economy by doing something. They add value by creating and consuming a wide range of products or materials, manufacturing, servicing, collecting and distributing, trading, entertaining, educating or building for the future. They buy from and support a ring of suppliers, large and small. There is in effect an outcome or series of outcomes, all of which have some use, meaning, or worth. Very few companies could get away with producing something nobody needs or values. This maturity of connectedness is the very core of purpose and meaning and brings with it a sense of identity and real responsibilities.

[‡] Jackman, D. July 23rd, 2012. *Extract from a Leader Article in the Independent Newspaper.*

CHAPTER 12

Place, Purpose, and Meaning

The Meaningfulness of Work

Working with or for organizations makes up a significant part of most of our lives, and our attitudes toward work and how we operate collectively through organizational structures, raises a mirror to determinations of wider social purpose and shared meaning. Corporate maturity is a holistic model for directing and evaluating the purpose of organizations and the meaningfulness of work. This is a difficult area and so we found it necessary to carry out some original research for this book to assist our discussion.

Commentary about work, "the blank patch between one brief evening and the next,"[*] is nothing new. In Wordsworth's pastoral poem, *Michael*[†] is broken by industrialization's erosion of the bonds between community toil and honest landscape—"I wished that thou shouldst live the life [our ancestors] lived." While Suzon's stare in Manet's *A Bar at the Folies-Bergère*[‡] incriminates us all in her commoditization and interrogates our very act of observation.

In the 1980s Dolly Parton reflected work as "*a rich man's game* ..."

Workin' 9 to 5, what a way to make a livin'
Barely gettin' by, it's all takin' and no givin'
They just use your mind and they never give you credit
It's enough to drive you crazy if you let it[§]

---

[*] Grint, K. 1998. *The Sociology of Work*, 1. Polity Press, first published 1991.

[†] Wordsworth, W.M. *1800 Courtesy of The Wordsworth Trust.* Grasmere.

[‡] Manet, E. *A Bar at the Folies-Bergère* 1882 Courtesy of The Courtauld Institite.

[§] *Nine To Five* from the film of the same name 1980.

While by 2016 Kate Tempest's performance poetry sees:

We have learned nothing from history
People are dead in their lifetimes
Systems are huge
The traffic keeps moving, proving there's nothing to do
It's big business baby and its smile is hideous
Top down violence, a structural viciousness[¶]

The Purpose of Organizations and the Meaning of Work

When and how any suggestion that work might have some "purpose"—a goal or direction—or give some degree of "meaning"—a value contingent on connections in a broader context—is unclear, but these themes have emerged from a number of partial perspectives:

1. Individuals—The producers of work—in developed economies might, for example, consider meaningful work to be a "must-have" accessory in their "quality of life" package. To the textile worker in Dhaka or rickshaw puller in Delhi, this may seem a risible luxury, a skittish self-indulgence of Maslow's[**] "higher-order" pursuits—of personal identity, self-expression, realization, happiness and self-fulfillment. The rickshaw wallah may not appreciate the irony, but self-fulfillment through work may represent a new form of oppressive ugliness of a self-serving, narcissism drawing millennials and beyond into a constant or virtual "act of becoming"—"an ongoing project of self-hood."[††] This "selfie generation," worse, may justify an entitlement, "*Because I'm worth it.*"[‡‡]

¶ BBC 2 *Let them eat chaos* 1.10.16.

** Maslow, A.H. 1943. "A Theory of Human Motivation." *Psychological Review* 50, no. 4, pp. 370–96.

†† *Inwardness: The Rise of Meaningful Work* 2008. Provocation Series Volume 4 Number 2 Stephen Overell.

‡‡ L'Oreal. http://lorealparisusa.com/en/about-loreal-paris/because-youre-worth-it.aspx

2. Employers—The consumers of work—may contrive a value in meaningful work as a method of delivering incremental improvements in productivity, loyalty, and retention. This may be no more than any other human resources management tool designed to deliver marginal returns, clothed in the language of employee engagement or job satisfaction—or, more cynically, in the bureaucratic version of "making a difference." This mere manipulation is pure "Apprentice-speak"[§§]. Digital technologies offer the potential to accelerate an appropriation of the authentic and the commitment of "heart and soul." This can also occur at the level of the state; "a Smart Nation is one where people are empowered by technology to lead meaningful and fulfilled lives."[¶¶] But while meaningfulness can be reduced to a means to a business end—are we not "just kicking the can of meaning down the road … *something* must be desirable on its own account."[***]
3. Communities—The context in which work occurs—affect and are also affected by the commitment, purposefulness, care, and intent with which it is carried out. The net of meaningful work may well be more than the sum of a more distracted, mundane activity; and moreover, the meaningfulness of that work may in part be derived directly from the impact on, and contribution to, the wider community and the environment.

We consider here:

(a) *What* are these connections?
(b) *How* connections are embedded?
(c) *Why* these connections have value?

---

§§ http://theguardian.com/news/2016/apr/13/how-boots-went-rogue

¶¶ http://smartnation.sg

*** David H. 1975."Enquiries Concerning Human Understanding and the Principles of Morals." In eds. L.A. Selby- Bigge and revised by P.H. Nidditch, 293. Clarendon Press.

Research

1. A survey of 98 employees of financial services firms in the UK, Singapore, and Malaysia was undertaken by the author in small groups, following a wide-ranging discussion, using the questionnaire in Annex A. Those surveyed were at a middle management level, sufficiently senior to have a strategic view and yet not so obliged, perhaps, to have rehearsed corporate answers. This followed a "ground up" approach, starting with a pilot survey of 11 UK firms and evolving the questions and options during the process. Where possible the results are combined but in some cases where the questions changed the results are out of 98.
2. Interviews with a contrast group of employees in sectors closely connected with the community or environment, such as farming and not for profits.

Is There a Connection Between Purpose and Meaning?

Respondents seem to have found it difficult to relate to the concept of purpose that the idea of meaningful work and, in particular, struggled to see purpose in ways beyond financial return. Fifty-one percent conceived of organizational purpose and 69 percent saw individual purpose in terms of benefits for the employer, primarily as financial return. This may be a reflection of the financial services sector, although 48 percent did see the primary purpose of the organization in terms of some form of benefits for the community or wider stakeholders and 69 percent understood any "worthwhile" element of purpose in community terms. Responses to the questions on purpose were categorized according to the perceived primary focus of being a "purpose-driven organization"(See Table 12.1 and Figure 12.1):

Table 12.1 Responses to questions on the purpose of work

	Individual %	Employer %	Community %
Q1. What is the *purpose* of your organization?	1	51	48
Q2. Why is this purpose *worthwhile*?	4	27	69
Q3. What is the purpose of *your* work?	11	69	20

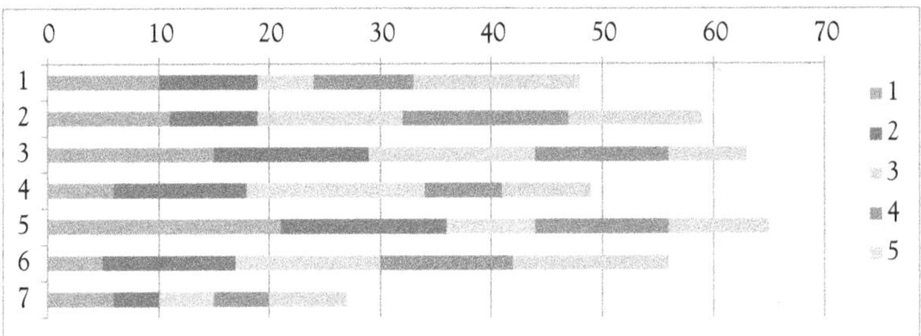

Figure 12.1 Responses to sources of the meaningfulness of work

See the following key:

1	Association with corporate purpose, values, or brand	Employer
2	Feeling part of a "team" or family	Employer
3	Worthwhile outcomes or a "good" cause	Community
4	Adding to prosperity, innovation or job creation	Community
5	Empowerment or learning and self-determination	Individual
6	Respect among peers or socially	Individual
7	Leaving a valuable legacy	Individual

Respondents seemed more comfortable with community dimensions of meaningfulness:

The association between meaningfulness and corporate purpose did not appear to be particularly strong in this survey. The connection between purpose and meaning seems to be indirect, in that both purpose and meaning derive, in large part, from a connection with the "external" community or environment. This external connection appears to be clearer to the employee in relation to an internalized meaning about their work than when considering a more distant and abstract purpose for the organization.

Can Meaning Be Managed?

It seems from previous studies that the enhancement of meaning at work by organizations can have a transformative effect on commercial success.[†††]

[†††] Peters, T., and R. Waterman. 1982. *In Search of Excellence: Lessons from America's Best Run Companies*, 323. Harper and Row.

Meaningful work can be highly motivational, leading to improved performance, commitment, and satisfaction[‡‡‡] and can lower business costs such as absenteeism, tardiness, turnover, labor disputes, sabotage, and poor quality.[§§§] More recently, meaningfulness has been evaluated as more important to employees than any other aspect of work, including pay and rewards, opportunities for promotion, or working conditions.[¶¶¶]

Our survey amplifies the focus on employee perception and highlights the following effects of meaningful work on firm performance.

Our survey ranked the perceived effectiveness of the methods by which organizations could try to enhance meaningfulness (See Table 12.2 and Figure 12.2).

Responses included both positive and critical observations of interventions to identify with place and belong to community which we might refer to as shaping the organization's and the work's "authenticity":

1. By allowing employees to challenge and question the way certain activities are carried out allows open communication or "open door" policy between employees and management (response number 6).

Table 12.2 Benefits of meaningfulness to the business

Benefit to firm	Number of mentions
Do you think meaningfulness improves employee retention?	9
Would you recommend organization to others?	11
Do you think meaningfulness improves the quality of work?	26
Do you think meaningfulness improves commitment to the organization?	43

---

‡‡‡ Pratt, M.G., and B.E. Ashforth. 2003. "Fostering Meaningfulness in Working and at Work," In *Positive Organizational Scholarship*, eds. K.S. Cameron, J.E. Dutton, and R.E. Quinn. San Francisco: Berrett-Koehler.

§§§ Work In America: Report of a Special Task Force to the Secretary of Health, Education and Welfare; WE Upjohn Institute for Employment Research, MIT Press, 1973.

¶¶¶ Cascio, W.F. 2003. "Changes in Workers, Work, and Organizations," In *Handbook of Psychology*, vol. 12, chap. 16, ed. W. Borman, R. Klimoski, and D. Ilgen. New York, NY: Wiley.

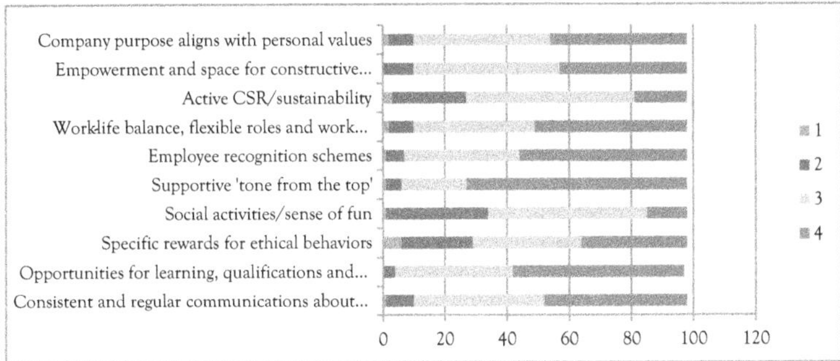

Figure 12.2 Interventions that increase meaning

2. The company provides training on its values but does not attempt to align with individual values and purpose. There's too many individual in the company to consider (15).
3. By informing us and emphasizing the company's purpose and values and providing a platform for employees to question "why" if there are any questions. By understanding why it would better help employees to align with their own values (20).
4. The company has tried to "sell" the corporate values to staff in order to promote positive outcomes (propaganda) (82).
5. Unfortunately it doesn't and that's why I have tendered my resignation (21).

It is observed that poor management can effectively and rapidly undermine any sense of purpose or meaning, especially by failing to lead by example.

Connections with Community

So how do such connections "bolt 'whole life' issues onto the world of work"?**** Meaning coming not just from the activity per se but from its impact on the wider world may arise from both "experiencing reality by interacting authentically with the environment and with

**** *The Good Worker*, The Work Foundation, 2006.

others, and giving something back to the world through creativity and self-expression."[††††]

Some responses indicate the nature of this connection:

1. We have launched insurance plans which are specially designed to cover the underprivileged (65).
2. Part of a collective effort o making society a fairer one (70).
3. Part of my responsibility as a citizen (82).
4. There are company policies that allow you to volunteer for the society. Be able to speak up for the better (86).

That is not to say that the activity of work does not provide meaning for employees. The European Foundation for the Improvement of Living and Working Conditions lists four key dimensions of good work: ensuring career and employment security; maintaining and promoting the health and well-being of workers; developing skills and competencies; and reconciling working and nonworking life.[‡‡‡‡] However,

> the search for meaning can be seen as that yearning for a feeling of wholeness and harmoniousness with the world, between day-to-day activities and some overall, animating purpose that gives direction to life as a whole. In becoming more of themselves they transcended themselves, becoming concerned with the self-actualization of humanity at large … when an individual perceives an authentic connection between their work and a broader transcendent life purpose beyond the self.[§§§§]

[††††] Frankl, V.E. 1959. *Man's Search For Meaning*. Boston: Beacon Press.

[‡‡‡‡] Eurofound 2001. *Good work paper*, 8.

[§§§§] Bailey, C., and A. Madden. October 2015."Time Reclaimed: Temporality and the Experience of Meaningful Work," Work, Employment, & Society. doi:10.1177/0950017015604100 Meaningfulness is therefore different from engagement, which is defined as a positive work-related attitude comprising vigor, dedication, and absorption. See Schaufeli, W.B. 2014. "What Is Engagement?," In *Employee Engagement in Theory and Practice*, eds. C. Truss, K. Alfes, R. Delbridge, A. Shantz, and E. Soane, 15–35. London: Routledge.

Corporate Maturity As a Framework for Evaluating Meaningful Work

Respondents categorized their firms within a corporate maturity level in terms of meaningfulness of work (Figure 12.3):

Minimum standards

- *Common question: Tell me what I have to do?*
- *Repetitive transactional; get the job done, no questions, no sense of "why?"*
- *Simplistic, short-term financial goals for all, shareholder value excuse.*
- *Oppressive and rigid hierarchical command structure.*
- *Cynicism, do as I say not as I do.*
- *Disenfranchising, don't take initiative, abdicate decisions or responsibilities.*
- *Little or no connection with outcomes or purpose.*
- *Alienating, undervalued, no desire to go extra mile.*
- *No local connections or sense of place.*
- *Turnover high, disposable staff on zero-hour contracts.*

Compliance culture

- *Common question: What must you do?*
- *Unthinking, mechanical compliance ticking boxes for comfort.*
- *Routine treadmill—dysfunctional silo mentality.*
- *Bureaucratic justifications and rote risk management.*
- *Reactive to external pressures, firefighting; a culture of dependency on regulatory permission.*
- *Frustrating lack of direction, unsophisticated measures of success.*
- *Disconnect between board and frontline reality.*
- *Fear infected- distributed sign-off to avoid accountability.*
- *Time-serving—kept in the dark, petty rivalries, little thanks.*
- *"Outsourcing conscience" to regulator or consumer.*

Business improvement

- *Common question: What can I get out of this?*
- *Tokenism and posturing—vulnerable—gap between fine words and everyday reality for staff and customers.*
- *Dull followers not leaders, incessant consultants' "benchmarking."*
- *Improvements only based on a business case.*
- *Self-regarding and self-justifying bubble of complacency.*
- *Overexposed, vanity projects, pay inequalities.*
- *Education secondary to competence "needs."*
- *Ethics equates to a marketing edge, little integrity.*
- *Staff policies and pay only to manipulate a result.*

Values led

- *Common question: What do we want to do?*
- *Independent judgment, internalize core values.*
- *Spirit not just letter, beyond compliance.*
- *Stakeholder balanced—long-term quality outcomes.*
- *Well-developed individual responsibility, empowerment and a sense of engagement by all staff.*
- *Space to make and own decisions.*
- *Wise, inspiring, "good" governance.*
- *Sustainable and resilient, excellent environment.*
- *Staff loyalty, engagement, and motivation adds value.*
- *Attracts best quality joiners, flexible working patterns.*
- *Celebrates innovation, flexibility, diversity, and learning culture.*
- *Worthwhile and clear purpose, answering the question "why?"*

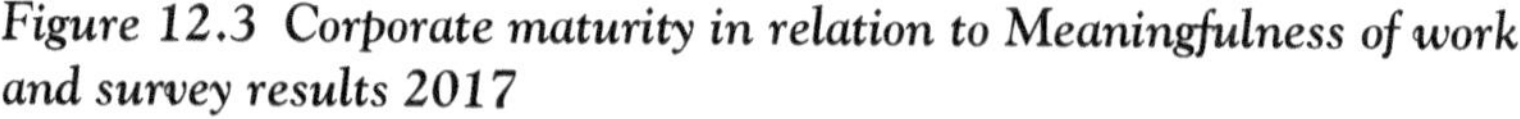

Figure 12.3 Corporate maturity in relation to Meaningfulness of work and survey results 2017

The aforementioned schema describes the four stages of corporate maturity in term of meaningfulness of work (version used in survey in 2017). The stages are, as before, not watertight or mutually exclusive, but show a general set of characteristics that may be true of a group or part of a group. They are typified by *attitudes* to work as an indicator of deeper conditions. Corporate maturity, as we have noted before, is a journey or direction of travel rather than an end, providing "purpose" by virtue of the progress experienced and the consequent meaning for the process engaged.

Connecting with Work and the Organization

Employees seem to find it more problematic to relate to the more distant prospect of purpose than the more immediate apprehension of meaningful work. However, it appears that there are linkages between two at a practical and implementational level. The engineering of meaning might bring marginal results for a firm, but the authenticity of internally generated meaning may be based more on connections with the world outside work, in rootedness in the community and environment, "the deep calls unto the deep." [¶¶¶¶]

Wherever possible people at work are exercising "a sense of redemption, a source of challenge or enjoyment, or the ability of the work to confer or reinforce social identity or identities."[*****]

> If employees don't care about their organization, and feels they aren't cared for in return, then their time at work is soulless... The workplace is the most natural environment for us to learn more about ourselves and interact with the world and people around us.[†††††]

The ILO (International Labor Organisation) Declaration of Philadelphia of 1944 states that "All human beings, irrespective of race, creed, or sex have the right to pursue both their material wellbeing and their spiritual development."

¶¶¶¶ Burton, Neil 2012 and 15 https://psychologytoday.com/blog/hide-and-seek/201205/mans-search-meaning

***** Baldry, C., P. Bain, D. Bunzel, G. Gall, K. Gilbert, J. Hyman, C. Lockyer, A. Marks, D. Scholarios, P. Taylor, and A. Watson. 2007. "The Meaning of Work in the New Economy." *ESRC Future of Work Series*, ed. P. Nolan, 40. Palgrave MacMillan.

††††† David Fairhurst in People Management, December 23rd, 2005.

> Too much reality, often heard in organizations in terms such as "let's get real here," deflates ideas and possibilities, but … inspiration without reality is experienced as pretence or as inauthentic and alienates from self, each other and the organizational purpose.[‡‡‡‡‡]

Essential to the connection with "other" is an element of unconditionality as we will see again with reference to authenticity. We found that vocation, community and public service are based on self-sacrifice,

> it subsumes the self into a community of disciplined practices and sound judgment whose activity has a meaning and value in itself, not just in the output or profit that results from it … A calling links a person to the larger community, a whole in which the calling of each is a contribution to the good of all.[§§§§§]

For Ruskin this unconditionality is expressed in craftsmanship:

> the lamp of sacrifice, by which he meant the willingness to do something well for its own sake; the lamp of truth, the embrace of difficulty, resistance, and ambiguity; the lamp of power, tempered power, guided by standards other than blind will; the lamp of beauty, found in the detail of things and people; the lamp of life, life equating with struggle, energy, and death; the lamp of memory, the guidance provided by the time before machinery ruled; and finally, the lamp of obedience—obedience to the example set by a master's practice.[¶¶¶¶¶]

---

‡‡‡‡‡ Lips-Wiersma, M., and S. Wright. 2012. "Measuring the Meaning of Meaningful Work: Development and Validation of the Comprehensive Meaningful Work Scale (CMWS)." *Group & Organization Management* 37, no. 5, pp. 655–85.

§§§§§ Bellah, R., R. Madsen, W.M. Sullivan, A. Swidler, and S.M. Tipton. 1985. *Habits of the Heart: Individualism and Commitment in American Life*, 66. Berkeley: University Press.

¶¶¶¶¶ Ruskin, J. 1901. *The Seven Lamps of Architecture*. George Routledge and Sons.

It is perhaps echoes of this selflessness which underpin a meaningful connection. And in time the embedding of this selflessness brings maturity and commitment.

Purpose becomes maturity; and, as with meaning, for regulators and communities, commitment is everything.

PART III

Why

Beyond the business case drafted in Part I, we need to consider the "reasons" or imperatives that might take a company or organization from a Level 1–3 position (see Chapter 2) across the *turning point* to a Level 4 place— being values led.

CHAPTER 13

Regulatory Maturity

The first reason "why" comes from first, regulators' increasing recognition, as they mature (as a special type of organization), of corporate maturity of regulated firms being a useful holistic measure of regulatees' fitness and properness, conduct, and outcome. This is an argument for developing maturity because it is in the organization's best interest and so is little beyond the enlightened self-interest of a Level 3 position. However the argument here is that there is a second component to regulatory intervention that has an element of inevitability about it. Corporate maturity arises from a natural momentum arising from an engagement with a more sophisticated, principle-led and outcome-based approach to regulation—that includes regulatory techniques, especially consciously designing ethical spaces into regulations—that naturally will have the effect of "organically" developing corporate maturity across a regulated sector as a by-product of pursuing straightforward consumer protection and market regulation objectives.

The relationship between regulators and corporate entities is strong in certain industries and professions and so their role in developing maturity deserves special attention. The regulators' influence in both encouraging and, on occasions, hindering maturity depends a great deal on the maturity of the regulatory bodies themselves and whether the regulator's maturity develops "in-step" or ahead, or behind, that of the sector.

Regulators develop maturity over time in the same way as any organization, and this can be seen both in their effectiveness as organizations and in their relationship and essential influence on the wider sector they regulate (and beyond that to their consumer communities). In terms of maturity regulators typically start developing slowly, using at first relative straightforward techniques and objectives, supported by fit-for-purpose checks on regulatees' internal systems; but as they grow in confidence and experience, often responding to and learning from crises, they will usually become more sophisticated both in deploying a more mature regulatory "toolkit" and in developing the maturity of their internal culture and the relationship with their stakeholders and regulatees. The pace of maturity development can be fundamental in shaping the wider maturity of organizations in the sector and so an understanding of where a regulatory organization is positioned on the maturity spectrum provides a framework for considering how far and fast the sector can develop and what help or support might be needed. This chapter proposes using the concept of "regulatory maturity" as a holistic view of the stage of development of entire (regulated) sectors similar to that of individual corporate maturity.

A Model of Regulatory Maturity

Three elements of overall regulatory maturity are identified:

1. Effectiveness of the regulatory body in delivering its stated objectives, including the sophistication of the regulatory tools and techniques used
2. Maturity of the relationship between regulator and regulated, and other stakeholders
3. Integrity of the internal regulatory culture, including the degree to which the seven principles are embedded

These three strands are connected. As a regulatory body gains experience and develops a more complex set of methodologies, it is likely, for example, to focus increasingly on prevention. Preventative approaches normally require some attention to regulatees' maturity—usually, therefore by definition, their corporate governance, culture, and ethics. Outcome and community, as we have seen, are only now emerging as additional things to complete the picture. To be credible and effective in these areas a regulator it is necessary for them to develop their own governance, integrity, and ethics. This increased emphasis on ethics is likely to reshape the maturity of the relationship between regulators and regulatees. This evolution can be represented in a general model of the development of regulation* (Figure 13.1).

* Jackman, D. 2015. *The Compliance Revolution,* Ch 2. Singapore: Wiley.

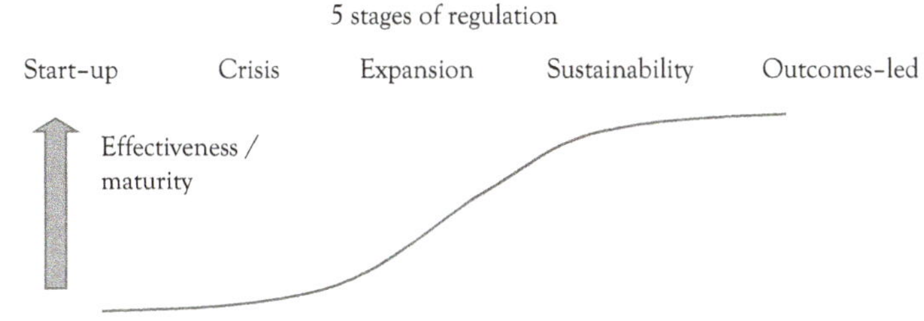

1. Straightforward tools for immediate effect and low-hanging fruit: licensing, capital, transparency	Shortcomings or gaps exposed as gaps exposed or unexpected risks crystallize	Ever-widening scope Risk-based approach Some tools address culture e.g., training and competence, fit and proper, fair dealing	Rule expansion costly Rationalization—key risks and prevention New focus on governance, culture	Focus on outcomes and conduct risk rebalances criteria away from systems and controls
2. Establishing credibility, policing role, enforcement led	Intervention or rules increase to restore confidence	Intrusive, costly and bureaucratic box ticking, visit cycle	Supervision proportionate from close to arms' length	Maturity evaluated allowing partnership, lower cost and risk
3. Operational, fit-for-purpose, but resources limited	Fire-fighting, opportunism and short termism	Increasing focus on process efficiency, benefits, and cost	Emphasis on ethics and culture in conduct risk	Common and holistic model of cultural maturity

Figure 13.1 Stages of regulatory maturity

This **Model of Regulatory Maturity**† helps to identify four levels of internal cultural maturity, each level reflecting the degree of connection with ethics, culture, governance, outcomes, and community (Figure 13.2).

The model provides:

1. A scale for evaluating internal regulatory culture
2. Direction of travel for the development of internal regulatory culture

† Adapted from Jackman, D. 2002. *An Ethical Framework for Financial Services.* FSA, London.

1. *Superficial*
    - *Question: How can the principles appear to be covered?*
    - *Fine words, some tokenism and posturing*
    - *Quick fixes*
    - *As little transparency as can "get away with"*
    - *Aiming for short-term results, limited ambitions*
    - *Industry or sector capture—sense of intrusion*
    - *Lack of confidence, vision, and security*
    - *Abdicates individual ownership*
2. *Procedural*
    - *Question: What do we have to do?*
    - *Unthinking, mechanical compliance*
    - *Dispersed decision making or decision sharing*
    - *By the book—black or white answers, ticking boxes*
    - *Bureaucratic and costly*
    - *Jobs-worth, inflexible application of principles*
    - *Culture of dependency on policies and procedures*
    - *Outsourcing "conscience"*
3. *Embedding*
    - *Question: How can we be more effective?*
    - *Making the business case*
    - *Reputational repair or building trust*
    - *Helps in delivering on objectives, not just a cost*
    - *Part of decision making at all levels*
    - *Staff give space to grow and trusted to make decisions*
    - *Judgment led*
    - *Public accountability and performance indicators*
    - *Long-term planning of developing principles*
4. *Values led*
    - *Question: What do we want to do?*
    - *Internalize principles*
    - *Spirit not just letter, beyond compliance*
    - *Well-developed individual responsibility and a sense of involvement by (all) staff*
    - *Focus on strategic stakeholder outcomes*

- *Good habit not audit driven*
- *Not looking over shoulder*
- *Knowledge sharing within and between sectors*
- *Leadership and innovation*
- *Continued reassessment and learning culture*

Figure 13.2 Model of regulatory maturity

Clearly, regulatory bodies do not necessarily mature at the same rate or exactly in the same way is their sector and there will also be periods of stagnation and regression brought about by external considerations and crises, but having this overall direction provides a consistent vision and direction of travel which is useful to the organization in its own right and its sector.

We have seen how ethics and cultural change is a complex matter and for regulators it is arguably even more complicated due to the expectations of society articulated through normal political processes and the requirements consult with or at least give consideration to the interests of all stakeholders. Each of these stakeholders may need to work together with the regulator to change assumptions, mindsets, and habits. This is a cumulative and cooperative process. No one is passive.

A Maturity Matrix for Regulators

Table 13.1 sets out the maturity of regulators in the form of a maturity matrix drawn from a public paper, by the author, for the UK Committee for Standards in Public Life (CSPL) as part of their "Striking the Balance report," published in September 2016.[‡] It sets out maturity in terms of the seven principles of public life, discussed in the previous chapter on ethics.

‡ https://gov.uk/government/uploads/system/uploads/attachment_data/file/553826/David_Jackman_-_Ethics_for_regulators.pdf

Table 13.1 Maturity matrix for regulators

Principles	Maturity levels Superficial	Compliance	Embedding	Values led
Selflessness	• Conditional—delivers "win-wins" • Acts for own benefit • Cynical manipulation • Low credibility or trust	• Rigid and bureaucratic • Rule following • Committee decisions • Resort to legal opinion	• Values led • See wider stakeholder aims • Live vision and values • Learning organization	• Inspiring commitment • Internalizing values as "way we operate" • Unconditional "spirit" See "common good"
Integrity	• Risk-managed ethics—deployed to advantage • Values reflect external expectations or political pressures rather than internal motivations • Regulatory capture • Ethics opportunist, faddish, eclectic • Contradictory actions and statements • Gap between board and frontline • Staff or public cynicism and disaffection • Ethics of convenience	• Compliant, to the letter • Avoiding any cost, inconvenience • Scope creep • Comfort from ticking boxes that avoid further thought or constructive challenge • Audit-based three lines of defense • Risk dominated • Cost-benefit analysis • Reactive firefighting	• Overly conscientious • Plenty of training • Toolkit approach • Outcomes led • Career regulators • Fit and proper test and financial show independence of office holders, boards and decision makers • Sometimes smug self-congratulation • Gifts and hospitality registered and limited • Revolving door issues	• Unconditional—applying principles even when no one is looking—even where they may be a cost or not contributing to any particular personal or organizational material benefit • Find the "right thing to do" • Internal compliance almost redundant • Limited people risk • Greater flexibility, creativity, and innovation • Space for judgments and owning imaginative solutions • Clear independence of financial position and career

Objectivity	• Everything "a good deal" • Possibility of preselected conclusions • Finding supporting evidence • Selective listening and restricted engagement	• Negotiated compromises • Well presented in media and externally • Influenced by strongest voices or parties with indirect or direct influence • Reputational risk uppermost • Evidence-based approach emerging	• Impartial—predetermined criteria for decision making, procuring • Decisions meritocratic • Zero tolerance on discrimination, prejudice or bias • Research based and objective data • Reviews independent	• Outcome driven—relating decisions to end user or consumer impacts and sustainability • Taking into account full range of interested and affected groups • Regard for inter- and intragenerational equity • Special attention to vulnerable groups
Account-ability	• Closed—limited appetite for accountability • Confidentiality paramount (which may be appropriate in certain circumstances) • Obfuscation by use of bland and general language • Small print mentality • Legal protections emphasized	• Legalistic • Not providing decision trail • Unclear roles, interests and responsibilities • Information released on a case-by-case basis	• Permeable—allowing insight into decision-making processes and participants, respective roles, responsibilities, reporting lines and eventual rationale • Sanctions publically taken • Open to public scrutiny	• Engaging—seeking to increase the amount of information publically available • Building capacity of the public to understand • Assisting media, education, and other dissemination bodies • To listen and test new expectations of accountability

Openness	• Shy—information released historically possibly only under pressure • Limited discloses, using jargon or inaccessible language or formats • Language restrictions • Use of small print and excessive length • Charging for certain types of information	• Transparent- disclosure in line with legal or industry requirements, exactly to the standards and levels or frequency defined • Unlikely to explain reasons for decisions in systematic way • *Note*: There are situations where it is lawful and necessary to withhold some information	• Accessible—makes available more than minimum levels of information in a variety of formats to suit different accessibility needs • Uses plain or clear language—to a standard that may be certified by a third party • Avoids any small print or excessive length • Uses assurance frameworks where appropriate and helpful • Makes valid cross-sectoral, cross-cultural, historic, and international comparisons where significant and helpful	• Proactive • Seeking out those who may have a reasonable or legitimate interest • Explain the implications of the information to the receivers • Educate interested parties over the long term about the issues that affect them, their options and their reasonable expectations • Feedback welcomed and the reasons given for deciding, acting, or responding in a certain way so that dialogue maintained and enhanced • Responses published with "answers" • Respondents listed or published

Honesty	• Relative—according to convenience and situation • Information provided selectively to support cause or personal advancement • Records altered • Minutes selective and circulation limited	• Record driven • Unclear as to what is not recorded, when and why • Contagion managed	• Truthful at a premium • Demonstrated by declarations, internal and external audit • Clear audit trails • Willingness to release information in timely and open way	• Honesty taken as a given as basis of integrity and professionalism • Any suggestion of wavering treated seriously and tough sanctions internally without needing external intervention or inquiry
Leadership	• Limited view of wider role or responsibilities • Short-term success criteria • Decision making confined to a few • Competitive view of peers • Confidential, isolated, and lack of information sharing or partnership • Follower	• Hierarchical and siloes approach • Leadership possibly tribal or territorial, may be for self-protection or advancement • Loyalty rewarded over merit	• Strong code of conduct and well-developed internal standards • Structure of constructive challenge embedded • Principles exhibited in individual and corporate behavior • Good examples documented, rewarded and communicated	• Strategic tone from the top • Willingness of all levels to challenge behavior and outcomes • Lower staff turnover and attractive to values conscious • Example to sector or peer organizations

The Influence of Regulatory Maturity in Developing Corporate Maturity

The original research for meaningful work in the previous chapter was extended to cover this area: In particular, to understand how interventions by regulators can trigger or reinforce management strategies within regulated firms with the purpose of aligning firm conduct more closely with wider community and social outcomes.

The influence of regulatory intervention on meaningfulness was easily recognized in this sector highly attuned to regulatory requirements (See Table 13.2).

In financial services the UK regulatory Training and Competence (T&C) regimes, for example, provide a framework of requirements for compulsory training, qualifications and CPD (continuing professional development) in all three jurisdictions. Training is a usual vehicle for delivering messages about purpose and meaning. The senior management and certification regime (SM&CR)[§] underpins the necessity for senior management to take personal responsibility, excise duty of care and show leadership, good governance, and "tone from the top." Regulators by requiring these systems and controls to be in place are supporting the key mechanisms of developing maturity. The dissemination of messages, rewards, and direction supporting maturity is not the purpose of these regulations but embedding maturity is a by-product of the regulatory agenda.

The regulatory aims, however, do align with one of the main components of meaning seen in the previous chapters. The regulatory aim of consumer protection is partly about narrowing the gap between the financial services industry and the communities it serves. Maturity can be expressed in the rules of regulators in terms of principles, as in the UK's Treating Customers Fairly (TCF) regime and Singapore's Fair Dealing

Table 13.2 Does regulation help or hinder maturity?

Regulation helps	Hinders	Both	Not sure
47	18	15	7

[§] https://fca.org.uk/news/press-releases/fca-publishes-final-rules-make-those-banking-sector-more-accountable

Guidelines, and these principles require firms to focus their financial advice, in this case, to achieve the following (more mature) outcomes:

Outcome 1: Consumers can be confident they are dealing with firms where the fair treatment of customers is central to the corporate culture.

Outcome 2: Products and services marketed and sold in the retail market are designed to meet the needs of identified consumer groups and are targeted accordingly.

Outcome 3: Consumers are provided with clear information and are kept appropriately informed before, during and after the point of sale.

Outcome 4: Where consumers receive advice, the advice is suitable and takes account of their circumstances.

Outcome 5: Consumers are provided with products that perform as firms have led them to expect, and the associated service is of an acceptable standard and as they have been led to expect.

Outcome 6: Consumers do not face unreasonable postsale barriers imposed by firms to change product, switch provider, submit a claim, or make a complaint.[¶]

Regulation can, therefore, be said to have an effect on increasing maturity, as an indirect result of policy makers and supervisors pursuing their consumer protection objectives.

The Potential Negative Effects of Regulation

Regulation, it should be noted here, reduces the need for organizations and individuals to think and to engage. "Just tell me whether I can do it." No understanding, no long-term embedding or education results. So regulatory evolution is vital for this cultural maturity to happen and we will explore this as a necessary parallel process in more detail. We shall see how rules-based regulation needs to move to a balance of principles and

---

[¶] https://fca.org.uk/firms/fair-treatment-customers and http://mas.gov.sg/~/media/resource/legislation_guidelines/fin_advisers/fin_advisers_act/guidelines/Guidelines%20on%20Fair%20Dealing.ashx

rules and recognition needs to be given to mature culture or good intent to move toward values-led culture.

So meaningful work can be enhanced by the intervention of regulation, but it should be noted that prescriptive regulation can act to frustrate the development of maturity by obscuring meaning, community purpose, and fogging the processes of collective learning and development. As established in part one, it is internalization of ethics and cultural standards that generates and secures maturity rather than the imposition of externally driven requirements.

How Corporate Maturity Is Useful for Regulators

An important question for regulators is how to ensure that change is effective and embedded. Much of this regulatory effort to connect external needs to internal processes started in the early 2000s[**] following as series of misselling scandals and was substantially accelerated after the 2008 global financial crisis when it was clear that, as President Obama put it, "the problems of Wall Street became the problems of Main Street."[††] Corporate maturity offers a holistic concept that is helpful in evaluating the overall culture of the firm, including within that the awareness of purpose, the meaningfulness of the work undertaken, and provides a broader-based "route-map" for directing the progress of regulation and firms, operating together, in improving consumer and community outcomes.

If regulators can measure corporate maturity it is possible to use this to determine whether a firm should be dealt with in a proactive and interventionist fashion or more as a responsible partner. In short it is possible to say whether a firm acts in a childlike way—responding only to being told what to do—or as an adult, foreseeing and avoiding problems for itself with minimal oversight. We can all imagine a naughty child in the back of the class being dealt with in completely different way from the well-motivated (and successful) mature student. Regulators and compliance can then tailor their interventions to improving that level of maturity.

** Jackman,D. 2002. *An Ethical Framework for Financial Services* Discussion paper 18. FSA, London.

†† https://whitehouse.gov/the-press-office/remarks-president-economy-georgetown-university

CHAPTER 14

Social Maturity

The second "reason" for developing corporate maturity is that it plays important part in developing a desirable level of wider social maturity (akin to community maturity), and which partly, and in turn, contributes to developing and encouraging corporate maturity.

What Is the Role of Social Maturity?

It is therefore a logical progression to suggest that corporate maturity is part of a wider social maturity. Corporate maturity, being maturity of businesses and organizations, contributes to the wider social process of maturing, while also being partly dependent on social development for its success and sustainability. The two go hand-in-hand and indeed may be mediated through the regulatory maturity discussed earlier.

Social maturity is potentially a large subject worthy of a second book, but an outline is given here using the same four-stage format as applied to corporate maturity to indicate how social and corporate maturity can develop hand-in-hand—and indeed are interdependent. The measurement of social maturity is very complex, but the community model set out in an earlier chapter would offer a good approach and at least an approximation. Society and consumers need to adjust what they expect businesses and organizations to allow them to develop. It may be that shareholder returns and pension expectations need to be systemically readjusted. The concept of shareholding needs reevaluation and different categories could emerge in terms of genuine long-term investment differentiated from speculation and income/capital gain. Also the function of work as a structure within which we meet some of our more fundamental human needs is emerging and may need explicit political and public support. In all these cases, the development of the collective narrative and the creation of what we have called "ethical spaces" and crucibles, deliberately and systematically, holds key to maturity in both corporate and wider social spheres. Is not, by definition, a competitive but a cooperative effort; and as the main global challenges emerge as inequality, climate change, managing urbanization and globalization, embracing diversity and meeting what we might call more "spiritual" human needs—it is clear that an international drive is required. The quest for authenticity is partly a reflection by individuals, generations, and certain territories of the need to directly address this agenda.

An Outline Model of Social Maturity

The following maturity diagram (Figure 14.1) is simply an overview of some of the consumer and wider social implications of a joined up approach to maturity:

1. *Minimum standards*
    - *Disconnected and unenfranchised, fractious and partisan*
    - *Repetitive transactional; get the job done, no questions, no sense of "why?"*
    - *Simplistic, short-term financial goals, shareholder value "excuse"*
    - *Rigid hierarchical command structure*
    - *Cynicism, do as I say not as I do*
    - *Little support for those in need, exploitative*
    - *Selective sense of international responsibilities*
    - *Little tolerance of diversity and difference*
    - *Little commitment, don't take initiative*
    - *Little or no connection with community outcomes or purpose*
    - *Alienating, undervalued, no desire to go extra mile*
    - *Little sense of community or sense of place*
2. *Compliance culture*
    - *Bureaucratic systems, open to corruption and abuse*
    - *Unthinking, mechanical compliance ticking boxes for comfort*

- *Disempowered, abdicate decisions/responsibilities, dependency*
- *Benefits culture costly and uncoordinated, sometimes abused*
- *Routine treadmill of low-pay work—dysfunctional silo mentality*
- *Bureaucratic justifications and rote risk management*
- *Reactive to external pressures, firefighting*
- *Frustrating lack of direction, unsophisticated measures of success*
- *Disconnect between vision and frontline reality*
- *Fear infected-distributed sign-off to avoid accountability*
- *Obfuscation, kept in the dark, petty rivalries*
- *"Outsourcing conscience" to regulator or consumer*

3. *Business improvement*
   - *Enlightened self-interest, meritocratic but not exclusively so*
   - *Wealth inequalities, restrictions to mobility and opportunity*
   - *Help means tested, divisive and uncompassionate*
   - *Tokenism and posturing—gap between fine words and everyday reality*
   - *Followers not leaders, dull incessant consultants' "benchmarking"*
   - *Improvements only based on a financial business case*
   - *Self-regarding and self-justifyingly—smug bubble of complacency*
   - *Inequalities seen as "part of the system"*
   - *Training driven by short-term competence "needs"*
   - *Ethics where useful, integrity convenient*
   - *Reward and recognition only to manipulate a result*
4. *Values led*
   - *Conscious and deliberate inculcation of "ethical spaces" into public policy*
   - *Learning culture and investment in liberal education at all levels*
   - *Citizens engage in discussion of difficult choices*
   - *Wide recognition that society cannot afford everything*
   - *Consumer education and responsibility*

- *Sophisticated regulation developing corporate maturity*
- *Balance of cooperation and competition, as appropriate*
- *Recognize and celebrate difference, yet common cause and values*
- *Value on independent judgment, accountability, and transparency*
- *Organizations led by internalized core values*
- *Spirit not just letter of laws and regulations, beyond bureaucracy*
- *Faith and beliefs respected and adding value*
- *Stakeholder balanced—focused on long-term quality outcomes*
- *Common kindness, care for vulnerable, hardship, and loss*
- *Leading international role, upholding human rights*
- *Unconditional individual responsibility, balancing rights, and responsibilities*
- *Driving out inequalities and prejudice of all kinds*
- *Flexible working patterns, meaningful work*
- *Celebrates innovation, diversity, risk taking, change, and exploration*
- *Treats "triumph and disaster the same"—people make mistakes*
- *Wise, inspiring, "good" governance and representation*
- *Sustainable and resilient, environmental management*
- *Deep appreciation of literature and the fine arts*
- *Gentle, self-deprecating sense of humor*
- *Authentic "spirit," answering the question "why?"*

© D Jackman 2017

Figure 14.1 Outline stages of social maturity

Obviously no society is perfect, it would be humanly impossible to exhibit all the features of the values-led level and certainly societies have a tendency to both improve and undermine themselves at the same time. What this schema provides is only a sense of direction and, crucially, its attempts to show that developments in levels of corporate maturity both contribute to and are facilitated by similar improvements in wider social maturity. For example, improvements in consumer education and awareness have an impact on corporate behavior and sourcing policies.

The interaction between corporate and social maturity is explored more fully in the next chapter.

CHAPTER 15

A Very Human Journey

The third answer to the question why offered here, relates to a wider philosophical view of the overall maturity of humanity. This takes the argument to a deeper level and provides the basis for understanding authenticity.

Philosophical Context

There seems few coherent answers to the current obsession with the neoliberal doctrine of Hayek and Freidman that asserts there is no alternative to objective market discipline and the only *reliable* attribute of human behavior (as Adam Smith saw it) is that we act competitively. Yet there is an equally powerful imperative within all of us that we readily recognize as another aspect of being human, that is to express our common 'humanity': grace, what we refer to as common kindness, equity, straightforward honesty, mutual care and respect, and even some humor and unconditional love. The problem is that many developed economies have sought to create economic, social, and political structures that allow for and promote the former without creating "space" for other equally valid human qualities to find their expression. Capitalism in and of itself cannot be said to have direction or character except that which we chose to give it, it is after all just a system, but our choices install within it mechanisms that make a more balanced approach difficult. In other words in-built assumptions such as, for instance, the capital accumulation of resources and power by a few make creating space for mechanisms that could promote intergenerational equity quite difficult. Thereby inequality becomes entrenched and exaggerated.

However, if we start from a more balanced set of assumptions then the role of business and the connection with community seems that much more reasonable and manageable. Let's assume for the moment that all human beings share the same basic needs and wants; everyone wants to be safe and secure, to be fulfilled, to love and be loved, to belong to a wider family and community. A predominantly competitive system and the practices associated with it accumulate and make the fundamental human aims harder to obtain. If we were to re-focus on finding ways to achieve these shared aims *directly and equally*, there would necessarily be less of a tendency to accept short-term 'solutions' such as mass consumerism and perpetual growth—both of which delude and deflect into accepting substitute goals. What is needed is a philosophical narrative and processes that recognizes the equal importance of other human goals. This is not difficult in conceptual terms and in the past Ruskin argued vehemently, if using terms we would now regard as archaic, for the restoration of such a human "balance" in work. The driving processes are the same as those covered in this book, the imaginative use of ethics, constructive challenge, triangulation, good governance, community outcome, and creative connections in the workplace: All of which are within us to find and to use.

We need to deliberately implant within all our collective systems, rewards and controls, sufficient "space" for the normal processes of human creativity, reason, and commitment to come to the fore and balance competitive pressures (in good governance, ethical business, progressive taxation, reporting, public spending, and education for example). It is the fine elegance and gritty realism of these spaces; their careful engineering and maturing that will foster and structure our humanity.

Three Journeys

Within these structures we can find and empower our shared values, and we may consider "progress" as three intertwined human journeys:

1. *A journey of being, belonging, and identity*
    - The visceral nature of the human trajectory: creation, growth, learning, discovery, death, and continuance

- Our sense of belonging to place and a locality, and an identity based on common heritage, shared experience and "rootedness."
- The narratives of "faith," and origin, success and tragedy, vision and end
- Prosperity and flourishing, self-actualizing, resilience and sustainability

2. *Finding "good"*
   - Discovering what is important, of shared value, ethics, and rights
   - Balancing conflicting interests
   - Making fine judgments or tough decisions
   - Disciplines of collective decision making
   - Concepts of "other" and shared purpose
3. *Joining with others*
   - Connecting in community
   - Economic mutuality and cooperation
   - Collectivity and kinship
   - Richness of culture and heritage
   - Understanding wider roles and responsibilities through good governance

Human maturity is the result of progressing collectively along these journeys.

This is not progress in the "grubby" sense of "purpose" or the mystical delusions of "destiny" but a practical model of the human condition in its entirety.

Crucially, this is a collective and not an individualistic endeavor. This is not about the vanity of self-justification, "because you're worth it," but describes the very journey of collective human maturity. This cannot be someone else's responsibility we must all recognize that we are involved as citizens and as employees or directors of companies. And we need 'others' to make the entire maturity enterprise successful. Only we can help each other in the process of giving and receiving good (ethics), being part of community, creating economies and belonging . We redeem each other.

Journeys for the Business or Organization

These three journeys may be considered in business terms to be connections with:

- Place
- Principle
- People

We have seen in the previous chapters how the following elements develop and interact and they fall into these three broad connections (Figure 15.1).

We discussed how an organization may "find good"—its ethics, values, and principles, what it considers important. We found how these ethics can be embedded in cultural structures and practices. We add the layer of regulatory intervention that can substitute for internal values if these seem systemically weak or underdeveloped, but which, if overly relied upon or overbearing, can create a culture of dependency from which it is hard to escape.

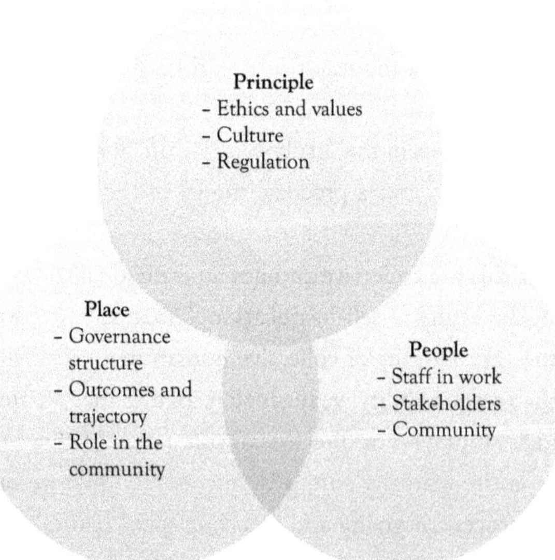

Figure 15.1 Three journeys

Then we explored the effect of actions on people both inside and outside the organization—the staff and the wider communality. How they are treated, involved, and listened to is crucial in determining and shaping maturity.

Finally (although in terms of the bigger picture this category comes first), we recognized the importance of "place," the role of an organization in a wider context. We found that the ultimate justification for an organization's existence comes from the "social license" or legitimacy given by the outcomes for the wider society or community. Governance is key in mediating the concept of place; and maturity, as a holistic concept, combines ideas of community role and purpose with the direction of travel or trajectory offered by the maturity model.

So maturity is a combination of all three of these crucial connections, working together, in the same direction.

CHAPTER 16

The Authentic Company

It is the depth of the connections explored in Chapter 15 that suggests a degree of genuineness and truthfulness we might describe as authenticity.

What are the fundamental differentiators that mark an authentic company? To answer this question it is necessary to build a deeper and more holistic view of the value and role of two aspects of maturity. This will also allow us to consider the further attribute of authenticity.

Unconditionality as Key to the Authentic Company

If it is the quality of the three journeys in combination with social maturity that creates maturity it is their coherence and *depth* that brings lasting and credible authenticity. This depth of maturity is what we might also describe as "being authentic" or genuine as it implies a degree of commitment in these connections, including steadfastness under pressure and in difficult or different situations.

A "test" of authenticity is often that these connections hold firm even when they may cost the individual or organization and are evident even when no one (such as a regulator, members, shareholders, customers, or the media) is watching or where laws and codes do not require a certain standard. This is the core to the concept on *unconditionality,* the preparedness to act in a mature way even if there is no advantage or self-interest. Unconditionality is the key differentiator in our model between Levels 1 to 3 and Level 4, values-led culture. In early levels organizations may choose to be mature because there is some marketing edge, cost advantage, regulatory dividend or reputational benefit. This is conditional; basing the organization's commitment on the "condition" of some return—a business benefit based on a business case. It is a deal—a "win-win." Whereas *unconditionality* requires unequivocal commitment, even when the decision or action may cost something or have no obvious benefit.

In other words, the organization does something because it believes it is the "right thing" to do. Crucial to this quality is that the commitment and the decision is made by the organization based on its own principles, because that is the way it wants to do things, rather than because an outside body such as a regulator requires or encourages it. It is about self-determination, responsibility, and accountability. These are the keys to maturity but also to the authentic company.

"Spirit" and Authenticity

There is a growing recognition that authentic and genuine business and brands have a certain authentic spirit. Many of the Y generation are attracted to companies that have strong social values and useful purpose. And as we saw earlier, meaningful work also has a value to many.

The spirit of any organization is often apparent to consumers and, particularly following the scandals enumerated earlier, looking for companies they can trust and those they can feel an affinity with, or are happy to be associated with. This affiliation may override price considerations and may include attention to sourcing provenance, working conditions, fair trade, and sustainability

If maturity is perhaps a direction of travel, then spirit is the encapsulation of a narrative to explain the value of the journey and a description of how to get "there" (or move forward). Principles, plans, and strategies are management tools to help translate theory into practice. But spirit implies some cause; usually beyond the simple interests of the company and goes beyond in the sense that the set of outcomes envisaged seem for a common good.

Companies often have purposes that are ultimately self-serving, it could be argued that any spirit that does not draw upon shared ethical values and meet wider human needs would probably not be seen as "authentic" and unlikely to get traction with some. Spirit needs to transcendental to the company's narrow interests and is inclusive, holistic, unifying, edifying, and parsimonious. Good purpose (and so implying the necessity of "good governance") makes the connection with common human purpose seen in Chapter 15—we redeem each other. This is what we see as "authentic."

CHAPTER 17

Conclusions

The high-level structure of this book has been to approach corporate maturity through a process of development elements or steps focused on:

- Ethics
- Culture
- Good governance
- Sustainable outcomes and community
- Place, purpose, and meaning

Having set out what constitutes corporate maturity in Part I, Part II outlines "how to" develop this maturity through the elements and stages necessary and the questions of "why" are considered in Part III.

Essentially, if maturity is about developing the three core connections described in Chapter 15, then authenticity is not only that but building a depth of connection in each case, as explored in Chapter 16.

Companies and organizations, just like people, struggle to bring together apparently competing demands of prosperity and fulfillment, of productivity and community. Yet they are entirely consonant and mutually reinforcing. Because regulators have come to represent the community interest, becoming industries' conscience, one side of the equation seems bureaucratic and rule bound while the other freewheeling and entrepreneurial. However, nearly every regulation is good "common sense" and entirely supportive of business aims.

Yet prosperity is a generative force... Far from eradicating risks, successful business is about understanding and harnessing those risks opportunities. Business could benefit from a deeper comprehension of the power of possibility. This requires a complex calculation of costs and benefits of community outcomes rather than, necessarily, finding good.

What matters is where an organization lies in this journey or "passage to maturity." Corporate maturity is, perhaps, just a reflection of and an essential part of a broader human journey. This journey is perhaps the essence of all human purpose, and so of corporate purpose, to build our communities, bringing humanity with sustainable prosperity.

We will leave the last word to Alfieri from Arthur Miller's *A View from the Bridge*:

> Most of the time now we settle for half and I like it better. But the truth is holy, and even as I know how wrong he was, and his death useless, I tremble, for I confess that something perversely pure calls to me from his memory—not purely good, but himself purely, for he allowed himself to be wholly known and for that I think I will love him more than all my sensible clients. And yet, it is better to settle for half, it must be! And so I mourn him—I admit it—with a certain … alarm.*
>
> *Curtains*

---

* Miller, A A. 1955.

Bibliography

By the Author

The Compliance Revolution, Wiley, Singapore 2015

Committee for Standards in Public Life (the Nolan Committee); *Striking the Balance* Paper on Ethics for Regulators and "Values-led Regulation" Cabinet Office 2016

Developing Sustainability for Communities ISO 37101 2016

(Guidance for Sustainable, smart and resilient cities and communities 37104 due 2018)

Ethics in banking, corporate maturity and faith, JISCC 2016

Sustainable Communities, Geographical 2015

Outcome Changes Everything, Journal of Business Compliance 2014

Resources Governance Index—numerous publications and articles—including in the *Financial Times, Scottish Accountancy, Business Week* 2009–2014

Social values, a leader in The Independent July 22nd, 2013

Good Governance—a handbook, ICA 2013

Guidance on Developing Sustainable Communities BS8904 primary author 2012

How Green a Games? Committee for a Sustainable London Olympic Games 2012

Ethics module RO1, Chartered Insurance Institute 2011

Ethics is the New Frontier, FS Review 2009

21st Century Charter 2009 and 2017

Handbook for Managing Sustainable Development, BSi 2007

Sustainable Development BS8900

Does regulation make it worse? 2004, Jnl of Financial Regulation and Compliance

Examination Framework for Financial Services Skills Council 2003

Examination Framework for Retail Financial Services 2002, FSA

An Examination Framework for Retail Financial Services 2002, FSA

An Ethical Framework for Financial Services 2002, DP 18, FSA

Examination Review, FSA 2001

Why Comply? Journal of Financial Regulation and Compliance 2001

Values-led Regulation, in Business Ethics, Economist Books 2001

Policy Statement 60, FSA 2000

Consultation Paper 60, FSA 2000

Consultation Paper 34, FSA 1999

Valuable People, City and Inner London North Training Enterprise Council 1998

Training Handbook, IMRO 1997

National Competency Framework for Investment Administration, The Finance Sector Training and Education Forum, 1997

Training and Competence Strategy for Administrative Functions, IMRO 1996

Professional Education, Securities Institute 1992

Other Sources

Doctrine Commission of the Church of England 2003. *Being Human: A Christian Understanding of Personhood Illustrated with Reference to Power, Money, Sex and Time.* London: Church House Publishing.

Financial Services Authority 2011. *The Failure of the Royal Bank of Scotland.* FSA, London.

McGilchrist, I. 2009. *The Master and his Emissary: The Divided Brain and the Making of the Western World* Yale University Press.

Parliamentary Commission on Banking Standards. 2013. A*n Accident Waiting to Happen*: *The Failure of HBOS.* London: House of Commons.

Reynolds, J., and E. Newell. 2011. *Ethics in Investment Banking.* London and New York: Palgrave and Macmillan.

Tolley, S. ed. 2013. *Banking 2020: A Vision for the Future.* London: New Economics Foundation.

Walker, D. 2009. *A Review of Corporate Governance in UK Banks and Other Financial Industry Entities.* London: HM Treasury.

About the Author

David Jackman has been at the forefront of designing aspects of financial services regulation, promoting a greater emphasis on corporate ethics and culture as Head of Ethics at the Financial Services Authority (FSA—now the FCA). He was primarily responsible for introducing the training and competence regime for the UK financial services industry, a system that has been adopted by many other jurisdictions. He cofounded a professional institute for market professionals and became the first Chief Executive of the industry-government Financial Services Skills Council. In 2004, David extended his interests to corporate governance and community outcomes, forming the Ethics Foundation and London Financial Academy and he currently holds a series of non-executive directorships in growth sectors.

As chairman of the British Standards Institution (BSi) committee for Sustainable Communities, he was primary author of the national standards for sustainable development (BS8900 – including for the Olympics 2012) and for Sustainable Communities (BS8904), now co-authoring the parallel international standards, ISO 37101 and 37104. David lectures, researches, and writes internationally, particularly in Singapore, and his recent publication, *The Compliance Revolution* (Wiley 2015) is a standard text. David has recently contributed to the UK Committee on Standards in Public Life's report on ethical standards for regulators.

David graduated from Keble College, Oxford University and Queens' College, Cambridge University, has been a Visiting Professor and a Visiting Fellow of Cambridge University Judge Business School. He lives in the English Lake District.

Index

OTHER TITLES IN OUR BUSINESS LAW COLLECTION

John Wood, Econautics Sustainability Institute, Editor

- *Preventing Litigation: An Early Warning System to Get Big Value out of Big Data* by Nelson E. Brestoff and William H. Inmon
- *Understanding Consumer Bankruptcy: A Guide for Businesses, Managers, and Creditors* by Scott B. Kuperberg
- *The History of Economic Thought: A Concise Treatise for Business, Law, and Public Policy, Volume I: From the Ancients Through Keynes* by Robert Ashford and Stefan Padfield
- *Buyer Beware: The Hidden Cost of Labor in an International Merger and Acquisition* by Elvira Medici and Linda J. Spievack
- *The History of Economic Thought: A Concise Treatise for Business, Law, and Public Policy, Volume II: After Keynes, Through the Great Recession and Beyond* by Robert Ashford and Stefan Padfield
- *European Employment Law: A Brief Guide to the Essential Elements* by Claire-Michelle Smyth